AUSTRIA

a culinary tour

Gerda Rob

AUSTRIA
a culinary tour

Including 75 recipes,
exclusively photographed for this book
by
Hans Joachim Döbbelin

Translation: Guthrie Thomson

SIGLOCH
EDITION

Title picture on page 2:
Austrian cooking is not merely a reflection of all that, through the centuries, has
become particular to each of the states. It has also claimed as its own many tasty
titbits from the once multi-racial state, adding only a certain Austrian tint.
Nonetheless, these often clearly remain imported products, given away by foreign
names. The countryside and towns of Burgenland, the youngest Austrian state,
display quite openly their proximity to Hungary. The photograph depicts a
farmhouse in Mörbisch by Lake Neusiedler.

© *1994 Sigloch Edition, Zeppelinstrasse 35a, D-74653 Künzelsau*
Reproduction prohibited. All rights reserved. Printed in Germany
Reproduction: Eder Repros, Ostfildern
Typesetting: Lihs, Satz und Repro, Ludwigsburg
Printing: Graphische Betriebe Eberl, Immenstadt
Paper: BVS chlorine free coated paper, 135 g/m²,
from Papierfabrik Scheufelen, Lenningen
Bookbinding: Sigloch Buchbinderei, Künzelsau
ISBN 3-89393-114-7

Eating Among Gourmets

Fortune, fate, or world history – whichever you choose – planted Austria's roots directly on the cross-roads of all the old European border paths. Looking down the millennia, this has been a noisy, shifting, fatally volatile, highly uncomfortable place. When any tribe of men, from the Mediterranean to the Baltic, from the shores of the Atlantic to the treasuries of the Urals, heard an urgent call to explore or conquer, this forested cross-road-land suffered the impact of the marching hordes. Always hard to bear, whether the hide shoes of the hunters, the Roman soldier's sandals, the laced shoes of nomads or the many, many generations of boots.

On the other hand, the original Austrians were perfectly situated: a central land – "surrounded by salt" – the rightly entitled "white gold". And, like all peoples bringing inherent and various possibilities, gifts and desires to history, Austrians also felt they possessed a strongly developed talent for trading, for change and for the use of power, that needed to be fulfilled. So they went rambling too, and not without success, as is clearly demonstrated by history. Nevertheless – and this is the positive aspect of the Austrian chronicles – they tended to prefer conquering with mind and heart, and less with the sword. At the latest since Kaiser Maximilian the clear maxim has been held, "Alii bella gerunt, tu felix Austria nube" – others may wage wars, while you, blessed Austria, must marry," and hence the Austrian family grew, with its understanding of life's varied pleasures. In this desire for fruitful love, admittedly accompanied by reason of state, foreign crowns, foreign legacies, and a dowry of foreign chefs were acquired. One example would be the Hungarian Stefan's crown. Another perhaps the Bohemian Wenzel's crown. They knew what they wanted and, in pursuit of acquisition and amalgamation,

worked constantly to entice new additions. The Habsburg Empire, still a world power at the beginning of the 20th century, consisted of 52 million people, sixteen cultures, a dozen languages and a dozen cuisines. In 1918 however, when this success was shattered, and all the glory disintegrated into a myriad of states, 45 million people receded behind the freshly drawn borders of a smaller Austria, taking eleven languages and eleven cultures into a freedom long desired by many. The only common legacies of these 600 shining years, were minorities, calamities and, on the positive side, the united cuisine of the Empire: Austro-Hungarian, Bohemian, Moravian, Croatian, Slovenian, Dalmatian, Bosnian, Italian, Romanian, Polish and Galatian cuisine.

No wonder in such a melting pot, that the Austrians have tackled the only pleasant part of their legacy with such eager enthusiasm, and, with the eye of a connoisseur, fished out all the *Gustostückerln* (tit-bits) from the wealth of different recipes. All the dishes have been given an Austrian touch, herbs added, and Austrian names or at least first names given, and they will never tire of proclaiming authorship until all of the world has been convinced.

Austria?

A Nation of Gourmets!

Josef Weinheber described so accurately the midday meal in a local pub in the magazine "Wien wörtlich":

"... A chicken broth so tasty
A steak in Madeira gravy
A pork pörkölt, venison ragout
Omelettes with some mushrooms too
Then a little Kipferl Cake
And a tiny tart for the road I'll take."

How did it all start?
It started early on!

There are few traces to be found of the early farmers' culinary habits, those who built the first permanent settlements on Austrian ground in the early Stone Age, between 5000 and 1800 BC. Nonetheless, we know that they were already using spoons made of clay, wood and bones around 2500 BC, that they caught fish, went hunting, were familiar with all kinds of cooking herbs and berries, and that they ate carrots.

It is only however circa 1000 BC that permanent settlements can be identified, where the Illyrer from the Hallstatt Age bartered with their salt for olive oil from the south, bred cattle, and sowed millet, barley and broad beans. They can hardly have been gourmets however, since, at the time of Christ's birth, their Roman Conquerors found local culinary habits simply barbaric. Cassius Deo wrote a letter home describing the then East Austrians in the Roman province of Pannonia: "They lead the most wretched of lives, with neither fertile soil, nor a good climate and no oil, no wine – or very little and of poorest quality – since for most of the year, it is so terribly cold. Millet and barley are their sources of food – and drink. But, they are the bravest people that we know, as irascible and bloodthirsty as their lives are devoid of pleasure."

Millet and barley were therefore the sources for all the *Sterze, Breie, Schmarren, Nocken, Nudeln* and *Knödeln*, and for the whole of Austrian cuisine, so rich in sweet dishes. Of course, our ancestors' menu did look a little sparse compared to their Roman counterparts. Just as Lucius Licinius Lucullus was holding notoriously extravagant meals in his villa near Tusculum, and at the same time as the Epicurean Marcus Gavius Apicius circulated ten volumes on the art of cooking,

Not only the town of Hallstatt, situated by a beautiful lake, is built on salt, but also many other towns in Salzkammergut.

when upper-class Roman gourmets were teasing their palates with oysters, truffles, crane ragout, numidian date chickens, turtle soup, fattened escargots and parrot brains, Austrians ate whatever the fields, forests and waters provided, devoid of culinary fantasy.

It was more due to economical considerations and less out of pity that the Romans began usefully to employ their five centuries on the banks of the Danube. They cleared large areas of land and transformed a wilderness into cultivated countryside. Vineyards appeared, fruit plantations were built, bees were kept. The first asparagus and first knowledge of exotic spices moved northwards on the heels of the Roman legionaries. One can almost believe their creation to have been idyllic. But history never remains idyllic long. Here also the signs had long been there for the reading, as, in the North and East, restless nomads began to move, driven by the Hun.

For six hundred years, between 375 and 976 AD, more than fifteen different races trampled every piece of cultivation right back into the ground. They burnt and robbed, murdered and plundered, then settled down in large groups on the apparently hospitable, useful land.

Only at the turn of the century was the situation redeemed, when the Babenbergers again made an attempt to create a country from chaos, and a people from this melting-pot of ethnic groups. Although then the terms *Osterrichi* and *Vienni* were used, one cannot think of an Austria like today. *Oserrichi* stretched from Linz to Hainburg and from Raabs to Semmering. To the South and West lay independent counties and duchies,

Was it beer, mead or wine, that the Austrians used in their "spirited" celebrations two thousand years ago, as shown on this beaten bronze vessel from Kuffern, by Herzogenburg in Lower Austria.

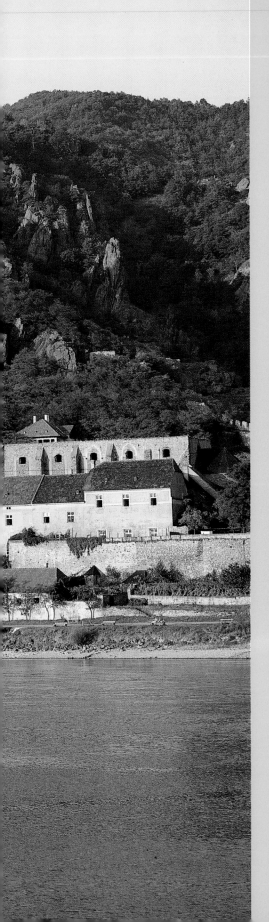

bishoprics and earldoms. It was truly an era of pioneers and consolidation. Monasteries and mighty castles high on the hills were built, the country became fruitful once again, and the population rapidly increased. Crusaders of the 11th and 12th centuries, moving eastwards along the Danube, praised the fine wine. Everything was prepared beautifully and bountifully. The mills, owned mainly by the monasteries, delivered outstanding bread flour, and, towards the end of the 12th century, the first professional bakers started to appear at market and in towns. In the "Fürstenbuch von Österreich" of 1227 is talk of *Kipferln* and *weiße Flecken*. Even then one differentiated between white and black bread. The aristocracy hunted passionately, wine-making extended beyond Austria's traditional wine-making regions, poultry was plentiful, and legal fishing rights were widely established and well-ordered. In the meantime, the Bambergers married, inherited, developed into a huge dynasty, and prepared the ground for the Habsburgs, who ruled Austria from 1282 until 1918. For the first time in 1438 Bohemia, Moravia, Hungary and Austria were united under one rule.

The manner of eating in those days, was described by Paolo Santonino, aide to the Bishop of Caorle, on a visit to Castle Finkenstein in Carinthia: "We were served eight courses: 1. Two fattened capons, stewed in their own juices. 2. One hare with numerous roast chickens and roast loin of beef. 3. Turnip and bacon. 4. Meat of young bear in a pepper sauce. 5. Cheesecake, fired in the pan with milk. 6. Hare meat, chicken trimmings and chicken liver. 7. Millet, boiled in fatty meat stock, served with numerous fat quails.

Whether Richard the Lionheart was served Kipferln and weiße Flecken, when he was imprisoned here in Castle Dunstein from 1192 to 1193 cannot be said.

8. A bowl of cream." And all that in 1486 ... It is possible, that we would not have enjoyed it all today, as, to dress everything magnificently "one adds cinnamon to the meat and a large quantity of cloves to the fish," but we have the Finkensteiners to thank for a particularly early pudding recipe: boiled rice, covered with almond cream, and garnished with almonds.

Around the turn of the 16th century, the culinary horizon in the Habsburger Empire widened at lightening speed. Maximilian, "The Last Crusader," Arch Duke, King and Emperor, married Burgundy's heir in 1477, and in 1494 the heir of Milan. The Franche-Comté, with its superb wines, was then also part of Burgundy, as was most of Flanders, and the important trading town of Bruges, and Brabant, Luxembourg and the provinces of Picardie and Artois. In turn, Maximilian's son Philipp married the Spanish heiress Joanna, hence not only acquiring Spain, but also the Spanish colonies, and Spanish lands in Italy.

Where eating habits in Austria previous to the rule of Maximilian had been humbler, based on flour, eggs, milk, a little meat, in the monasteries and castles mainly fish, wild game and poultry, life now changed dramatically, the starting-point was Maximilian's court in Innsbruck.

This Emperor, Renaissance man and gourmet, brought passion for refined pastries and tastebud-tickling sauces from the self-fashioned pinnacle of French gastronomy, Burgundy, from Flanders a love for sugared fruits, confectionery and conserves or jams, and from Italy the recipes of the Maestro Martino, who had resurrected the pomp of Ancient Rome among the gourmets of the Italian Renaissance, also were embraced Cinnamon and ginger, raisins and dates were used generously, alongside pomegranates bitter oranges and sugar. Italian pasta and rice dishes, and probably also a kind of fried cake – the predecessor of *Krapfen* – were known in Maximilian's capitol city Innsbruck, which he always preferred to Vienna Even if Maximilian had little success with his plan to import confectioneries and "put an end to the barbaric drinking," we can still view him as the bringer of haute cuisine to Austria, from whose wealth French haute cuisine also has profited. Only a little later, when the Dutch and Spanish *Zuggermacher* gained entrance to the Viennese palaces, every basic ingredients of the modern cuisine – barring potatoes – was assembled.

Far from the imperial kitchens and aristocratic tables, Austria's general populace also ate well. Nearly sixty recipes exist for preparation of conserves and purees, and suggest that these country folk still essentially ate what they produced themselves. However, the 1556 "Culinary regulations of a newly built hospital" gives certain clues as to an average menu: " Firstly, on meat days, generally throughout the entire year, breakfast should consist of meat, cabbage, bacon, and barley in a broth. Evening meals should be boiled or stewed meat, with sugar beet, or, during the summer, carrots or white turnips, depending on the season. Every alternate day add an extra piece of meat with coarse barley. On Sundays, celebrations, Thursdays, and the last day before Lent, instead of

When Maximilian I married Maria of Burgundy in 1477, and then Bianca Maria Sforza, heiress to Milan, in 1494, the flavours of the whole wide world entered Austrian cooking. Maximilian himself was a great huntsman, wishing to be the best of the entire Holy Roman Empire. A deer hunt on the lush pastures near Innsbruck is one of the three colour pictures by Jörg Kölderer contained in the Tyrolean hunting book written by Maximilian.

stewed meat, a roast. During Lent, broth in the morning, cabbage, and for each person a herring. If it is not herring season, then for every person one baked or two poached eggs and a milk pudding. For the evening meal, oat, suet or cheese pudding, turnip and on occasion a fish, boiled with onions, according to the season, or for every person one baked or two poached eggs and an oatmeal pudding. On special days in the summer, a salad with the evening meal ..."

It was also in the 16th century that the first Austrian cookery books were published. One example would be the hand written book of Philippine Welser, wife of Arch Duke Ferdinand II. The "Welserin," whose parties in Castle Ambras were famed throughout all of Europe, knew dozens of recipes for meat dishes, including thirty-six for pork alone. She served beef with horseradish, and indulged herself in tarts, pastries, cakes and almond milk. The thought that boiled joint of beef with horseradish may have originated in Tyrol is a nightmare for the Viennese. It cannot be denied, nevertheless, that Tyrolean cooking, according to historical influence, had edged several lengths ahead at that time.

During this period, the Viennese Royal Court underwent dynastic change. Karl V, son of Johanna of Spain and Philipp of Burgundy, united all Habsburg estates under the Austrian flag, thereby creating the most powerful dynasty in Europe. While the Turks camped before Vienna, Spanish Royal etiquette and ceremony was introduced within the Royal City. After this, tables were set according to Spanish custom with cutlery on the right hand side of the plate, and the Spanish pastry-makers and masters of the sugar from the Canary Islands grew to be well loved. The rest of Spanish cuisine however, remained unpopular, and, apart from the nutritious *Olla potrida* broth, made from a cross section of all kitchen ingredients and still found in nineteenth century Vienna, no recipe worth mentioning has survived.

It would seem that the great pleasure banquets reached their first pinnacle in the course of the 16th century. Feasts lasting several days were by no means uncommon since everyone wanted to taste all the new creations, to sample and enjoy every culinary achievement at once. Banqueting became so widespread that in 1542 Ferdinand I passed a decree dramatically reducing culinary luxury: Barons were only to be allowed forty guests at a banquet; knights, citizens and merchants twenty-four; and tradesman and freemen only sixteen. The decree had little success however. Royal culinary secrets were by now no longer confined to a tiny elite.

Barons and Counts wanted what the Emperor ate.

Rich citizens wanted what the counts ate.

Tradesman and farmers had enough of porridge, maize and mash.

Hence, the people preferred to ally themselves with the twenty eight year old Styrian Arch Duke Ferdinand, who, despite his age was already bon vivant par excellence, and who, as early as the start of the 17th century, had commissioned a 600 page cookery book, making particularly clear his passion for tarts and all other varieties of sweetmeat.

No, neither the Thirty Years' War, the plague, nor a second Turkish siege could spoil the appetite of those Austrians not directly affected. At the end of the 17th century, the Baroque King Leopold felt the divine call to guide his citizens at their tables. Not only dividing them into five groups, he also passed decrees proscribing which luxuries each classification could or could not afford.

Throughout the countryside, control officers searched kitchens and cellars for traces of ingredients that indicated a breach of the law. King "Wheatsearcher" and his band of wheatsearchers were determined, but not exactly successful. No more so at least, than the Augustine preacher Abraham a Sancta

wie man ain biber

schwantz sol ein machen

so nim den biber schwantz vnd die floen vnd brüe
zu biß die ober haut herab gat so nim zu vnd daß
die haut dar von vnd leg zu wider zu wasser
vnd seut in vn gefor 3 stundt biß er weiß wirt
zu wasser vnd wan er die ander haut laßt so
daus zu herab vnd mach zu saubern vnd darin zu
zu ain pfannen vnd geuß ain gutten wein darin
vnd laß zu sieden biß er lindt wirt als ain muß
wan er schier gesotten ist so daus safern pfefer
imber welang ain weing negela zuckder daran
vnd laß zu wol sieden vnd ain droepflin essig
vnd richt zu mit brüe vnd fisch an

How to boil a beaver's tail

"Remove beaver's tail and claws and boil until the outer skin peals away. Then remove, peel away skin and replace in the water. Boil for approximately 3 hours, until it turns white. Once the second layer of skin can be peeled, remove from the fire and clean. Place in a pan and add a good wine, allowing it to boil until soft like puree. When it is ready, add saffron, pepper, ginger, cinnamon, a few cloves and sugar, and allow to simmer again, and add a dash of vinegar. Then serve with sauce and fish."

This is a recipe from the hand inscribed cookery book brought by Philippine Welser in 1557 to her secret marriage with Arch Duke Ferdinand. Today it has been returned to her Castle Ambras near Innsbruck, famed for her banquets far beyond the borders of the country. Beaver's tail was regarded as a particular delicacy of Lent, since the beaver is a water animal and hence classified as fish.

Clara, whose Viennese pulpit sermons vehemently denounced the gastronomic Zeitgeist, the bands of bon vivants and dissipated consumers. In his eloquently argued pamphlet, "Revolution of the animals against the Gourmets," he wrote of "This well-known fiend called Consumus Enormous, the resident of Gourmet-town, native of grub-land, whose knowledge of gorging and riotous living is so great, his relentless paunch served by fowl of the air, fish of the ocean depths, wild beasts of the earth, in total, everything edible, and so damaging to his Soul."

Only a few years following this Royal and ecclesiastical admonition to moderation, the chef of the Salzburger Arch Bishop presented his "New Salzburger Cook Book," enabling one to "present and prepare meals of the most exquisite style for aristocratic and genteel courts, or for large gatherings of guests, and to provide common meals of pleasant daily variety."

Conrad Hagger's culinary work "Royal Roman Majesty Privilegio" contains more than 2500 recipes and long remained the classic text.

The exited report of J.B. Küchelbecker in 1730 is hence hardly surprising : "In Vienna, the greatest investment, both spiritually and materially, is in eating and drinking, whether of fine or basic quality, so that there can be no better nor enjoyable way of spending the best part of the day, than at table, with a glass of wine."

The prevalent influence of the 18th century was Maria Theresia, the Lorrainese wife who returned French habits to Austrian Royal kitchens. There were nevertheless few major changes, since recipes had been cosmopolitan for quite some time, with Italian cooking much loved, anything Hungarian by then almost Viennese, and anything Bohemian already swallowed whole.

Despite this, the regal housewife caused something of a revolution in the average kitchen. Influenced by almost void treasuries, she refused to allow Royal left-overs simply to seep away into the court, instead selling them to an entrepreneurial innkeeper. Soon, Viennese gourmets could feast on pheasant and capons, yeast noodles and roast quail at quite moderate prices. Female citizens, as the story goes, "screamed, fought and bit their way to the recipes."

But was this Queen not as frugal as all that? The state archives of Melk record a day-trip made by Maria Theresia which would be likely to leave a substantial hole in the accounts. In order to "Entertain her majesty and entourage" they required: 587 pounds beef, 743 pounds veal, 9 veal heads, 40 veal trotters, 33 veal breasts, 56 pounds pork, 78 pounds mutton, 13 lambs, 4 pounds ox kidneys, 4 pounds marrow and 4 ox tongues, 6 pounds coffee, 32 hares, 4 wild poultry, 11 eighths of suet, 1405 eggs, 15 trout, 6 pounds capers, 8 pounds large raisins, 6 pounds grapes, 9 measures of cinnamon, 7 venison, 1 chamois goat, 2 deer calves, 1175 crabs, 5 new roasting spits.

In addition to this, pastries, dumplings, noodles, vegetables and salad were served. If the absence of potatoes becomes apparent, then this is not without reason. Certainly they quickly spread throughout Austria's farm lands in the second half of the 18th century, first in the Vorarl Mountains and in Tyrol, but it was the cooking of the poorer people that brought them popularity. In Vienna, where the first potato plant arrived in 1588, production of potato spirits was first attempted, but only during the Napoleonic wars was the potato remembered as a vegetable side dish. And it was within the second half of the 19th century, with the creation of the first potato dough and hence dumplings, that they became truly popular.

With the exception of the Vienna Congress – recorded in the annals as the "Dancing Congress" – to which Napoleon's foreign

minister Talleyrand travelled with Antoine Carême, probably the finest chef of all time, and at which Chancellor Metternich spoiled his guests with exquisite inventions, there were no major changes made to cookery in the 19th century. Although there was now an abundance of sweet things, sausage recipes had been refined and tomatoes introduced to Austrian cuisine, and the bourgeoisie aspired to a certain quality of life, it was essentially of a more mundane quality: "fried chicken and roasts, smoked pork and bacon, goulash with capers, broths, dumpings, cakes and titbits."

In the second half of the 19th century, immigrants from all over this multi-racial state moved determinedly towards Austria.

Hungarian aristocrats brought gypsies and the Csárdás, paprika, goulash, finest fish recipes, paté de fois gras, strudels, semolina noodles, and the Dobosch cake.

Balkan immigrants brought a taste of the Orient, craftsmanship, the most famous caper recipes, a love of mutton, stew dishes and Turkish halva.

Vegetable soups were an innovation of the Italians, in addition to ravioli and macaroni, numerous spaghetti recipes, risotto, polenta, gnocchi, osso buco, fennel, zucchini, artichokes and chestnut cakes. From Bohemia came tailors and shoe-makers, tradesmen and servants, nursemaids and cooks. Their native repertoire was *Schinken in Brotteig, Schinkenfleckerln, Liwanzen, Schkubanken, Kartoffelknödel, Wasserspatzen, Serviettenknödel, Marillenknödel, Powidltascherln, Bohemian Dalken, Buchteln, Kolatschen, Grammelpogatschen* and *Zwetschkenröster*.

"When Bohemia was part of Austria" is the line in a well-known song, although "Bohemia" can also be interchanged with Agram, Lemberg, Cracow, Triest or Trient. It was approximately a hundred years ago, that the classics of the nation's cuisine developed, today inscribed as if in stone on every menu. Sifting the varieties of their multi-racial state, they kept the best for themselves. Austrians are the happy heirs to the cuisine of half of Europe.

Next double page:
During the reign of Maria Therese, a strong cultural and culinary exchange developed between Austria and Hungary, whose Stephan's crown had been worn by the Habsburger since 1526. Count Nikolaus Esterhazy engaged Joseph Haydn as Royal composer – here playing the piano during an opera recital – at his magnificent Castle, the "Fairy-tale Esterháza."

Blatteln, Wirler, Wefzgenescht, Grattler, Tommerl, Kaschernat

Nine federal states, nine small Austrias, nine regional dialects, and an endless variety in all. 7.4 million people, 7.4 million individualists with firmly set philosophies of life: heaven is found in the Vorarlberger Nenzig, you descend to hell in the Burgenlandian Podersdorf, Baby Jesus was of Upper Austria, choral singers inhabit Lower Austria, Tyrol is tops, Salzburg is paradise, Carinthia is Shangri La, Styrians are strong as oxen, and as for our Lord God, the Lord God must be Viennese.

One almost feels like quoting Friedrich Hebbel, a native of Holstein: "Austria is a small world, within which the larger holds rehearsals."

Given the extent of regionalism, in a country looking back on an almost two thousand year old café culture tradition, it is hardly a surprise that names given to foods and to the numerous recipes also demonstrate wide discrepancies. What do the Viennese know of the *Grantn* or *Granggn* that they call *Preiselbeere* – cranberries, what can the Tyroleans say of Burgenland's *Haadani Kneidl* that they call only *Schwarzplentene*, or what can Vorarlbergers say of the Lower Austrian *Saumoasn* and what do the Upper Austrians assume of the Carinthian word *Maischeln*?

"Ye'll hae tae twist yer tongue," wrote Joseph Binder quite correctly in his memoirs, "if ye move from one region to another, and nae only because o' th' pronunciation."

For sure.

The Vorarlbergers, being Alemannian, leant more towards their Swiss neighbours than towards Tyrol, from which they are divided by the Arlberg mountains, or the rest of Austria, which tended to be viewed like an East Pole.

The hard-working, conscientious country folk, whose dialect sounds like a mish-mash of Swiss German and Dutch to anyone other than a Vorarlberger, have often the sneaking suspicion that sausages called *Frankfurter* in Vienna, and *Wiener* (Viennese) in Frankfurt, were named *Zitzale* by themselves, so that they would never, even by a sausage, be reminded of the town to which their taxes disappear. They remain equally idiosyncratic in the kitchen. Specialities like *Käsesuppen*, *Schiebling*, *Moschtbröckle*, *sure Kuttla*, *Riebel*, *Tosche*, *Knöpfle*, *Spätzle*, *Zwätschger*, and *Kriesewasser* pose not only linguistic problems to the rest of Austria. Tyroleans, on the other hand, live and have lived primarily for Tyrol, including South Tyrol, which is now part of Italy. The "Holy Land of Tyrol," first so called in an operetta of 1796, and later in the songs of Andreas Hofer, has remained essentially pragmatic, despite huge invasions of tourists. Pithy, reserved, truth-loving, pedantically concerned about their independence, chauvinistic and amusing, would typically be attributed to the Tyroleans. But even their amusing side has a core of seriousness, as if echoing the favourite motto of Kaiser Maximilian, found on his chamber wall in Castle Tratzberg of the Unterinn Valley:

Live, I know not how long
And die, I know not when
Must go, I know not where
Strange, that I feel so free

Tyrolean cooking was affected by King Maximilian's Flandrian culinary culture, and by a geographical proximity to Italy. In Vienna, dishes such as *Weinsuppen*, *Weinbeizen*, *Schlutzkrapfen*, *Türtln*, *Profesen*, polenta, various forms of *Nockerln* and

Spatzen, Maibutter, Mandelsulz, Holler-punch and *Kranebitt* are completely unknown.

Salzburg joined Austria for the first time in 1805, and has remained since 1816, "an arrogant town in an arrogant land" that "made a lot of wind and burnt a lot of witches". It is today probably the most cosmopolitan of all the Federal States. Salzburgers have always taken time to enjoy life, seeing themselves as beer brewers, and conducting a coquettish love/hate relationship with their Bavarian neighbours. Without a doubt, that same joie de vivre lives on in the baroque city and its hinterland, where an Alemannian Arch Bishop built the "German Rome" by the Salzach, and the chef of another Arch Bishop wrote a gourmet cookery book, coyly including a few less expensive recipes, "for those only occasionally able to treat themselves, but still wanting to know how".

When, during the Festival, Salzburg raises its head above the others of the Austrian family, these others comfort themselves with the thought that also Salzburg has an "Everyman" to drag it back down to earth. In a culinary sense, the Salzburgers enjoy the legacy of their Arch Bishops. Hence they were brought together with haute cuisine a little earlier than the other, more remote regions, but also were distanced from most of their own culinary creations. With the exception of the *Salzburger Braten* (roast) and the *Salzburger Nockerln*, various purees, *Nocken* and *Strauben*, there are very few recipes that originated in this city.

Carinthia has often suffered during the last sixty years because of its border position, and is therefore understandably marked by strong nationalistic feelings, totally alien to the rest of Austria. Vienna in particular successfully coped with a quota of more than 60 percent foreign-language immigrants at the start of this century.

These "sharp, world weary, sensuous and intellectual" Carinthians, holding the world record for illegitimate births, are also the sarcastic clowns of the nation. Villachers cover Klagenfurters with pointed mockery, and the Klagenfurters pass this in turn to their Styrian neighbours. Usually however, they are not in earnest. Even on the occasion when a British officer climbed the landmark of Klagenfurt, the lindworm refrained from snapping at him with its many teeth, instead breaking off only the peak, hence allowing the unworthy weight to tumble gracelessly to the ground. Carinthian cooking is in keeping with the farming land, ungainly but flavoursome, and never be taken in by the delicate diminutives used. The *Maischelen*, their *Spatzlan* and *Leberlan*, the *Miaßl*, *Blattlan*, the *Reinngalan* and the *Niggelen* are all decidedly rich foods.

The green land of Styria, often and falsely described as Rossegger's forest home, is divided into mountain, valley and hilly landscapes, some areas so isolated that the inhabitants are almost locked away in a cell, and hence are so unique, that it becomes difficult to call them Styrians: the pensive, careful Mur Valley dwellers sit next to the staunchly conservative Enns Valley people; charming Ausserian women are found in the centre; weather-beaten dairymaids from the Nock Mountains and the agile, up-to-date Grazerians will also be encountered; and then there is the East Styrian, with his love of life; and the gentle, passionate Lower Styrians, who never totally renounce kinship with the Slavs. The one thing uniting them is

Next double page:
Maximilian's Chamber in Castle Tratzberg in Tyrol – the way of life of king and man 500 years ago.

musicality, the joy of singing, the lust to make music, and the Styrian custom.

People enjoy referring to them as generous and comfortable, and praise Styria as a place for the summer angler, the bourgeoisie and holiday visitor. You would however, be surprised to note that it was exactly here that the avant garde Austrian poets were born, grew up, and sometimes enjoy a little fool's paradise. The cuisine varies as much as the landscape. Instead of a general consensus, they have only a collection of the specialities of tiny regions, although one might mark the recurrence of thick soups and substantial broths, of bean, pumpkin and wild oat dishes, of *Sterze*, *Tommerl* and *Krapfen*, as well as all varieties of ginger-bread and sweetened bread.

Upper and Lower Austria, the Austria "above and below the Enns," are the heartlands, the centre of this feudal, inherited land, the home of the ruling Habsburg dynasties throughout the centuries. It is a continuous, rolling, fruitful landscape, without enclaves of foreign settlers, where one can live quietly and unobtrusively.

Friedrich Sacher once wrote of Lower Austria: "You have never risen to be much, but you are faithful and constant. You were never childlike, but neither need you grow older ..." Lois Schifferl expressed in his own unique way, a similar thought about Lower Austria: "No Viennese big-mouths, no arrogance, no swindling and no tantrums." This of course clearly demonstrates the

Two hundred years ago, the grocery women of the Green Market in Salzburg enjoyed a free concert, as the young Wolfgang Amadeus Mozart practised the piano in his parent's house.
Next double page: The Enns and the Reichenstein rush together. After leaving the Steiermark, the Enns winds its way northward between Upper and Lower Austria.

prevalent attitude towards Vienna, the "arrogant capital", which felt the urgent need to create its own Federal State right in the middle of Lower Austria. But it does not mean that Upper and Lower Austria have always maintained a warm, heartfelt relationship.

Certainly they are divided in their beverage preferences. Whereas one tends to drink beer and eat beer sauces in the Innviertel, in Upper Austrian Traunviertel the preference is for cider – and cider sauces – and the lower Austrians of course drink wine and eat milk soup ...

The Traunviertler are to blame for the nickname common to all Austrians – *Most-schädel* or cider heads. Occasionally intended as a term of respect, meaning steadfastness, defiance, firmly-planted and self-confident, it can also be used in derision to mean stubbornness, obstinacy and immovability. But this never bothers the Austrians, who wear it like an award. An Upper Austrian mayor once even wrote a poem to "The Cider Heads".

Whoever makes merry with cider and beer, also of course needs *Oarkas*, *Kochkas*, *Oar-fisch* and *Tsöan*, he needs salsifiers and radish salad. Excepting *Zaunerstollen* and *Ischlerkrapferln*, created by one baker, few others of the specialities of this regions cooking like *Knödeln*, *Nocken*, *Nudeln*, *Schmarren*, and *Strudeln* have been integrated into Austria's general cuisine.

Lower Austrians naturally stick to their wine. More than 250 years ago, Probst Hieronymus Überbacher wrote of them, not without a certain wry mockery:

A view of Vienna and St. Stephan's Dome, the former centre of life for the Danube Monarchy. It is hardly surprising that the Viennese continue to believe "the Lord God must be Viennese."

... if I should die and have to leave this place,
May wine be my last drop and my last spoken trace,
And let it be written on that gravestone o' mine,
Wine, wine, wine, wine, wine, wine, wine, wine, wine, wine.

In addition to wine, Lower Austrians are a dab hand at preparing fish, and numerous good recipes originate from the banks of the Danube. Proximity to Bohemia has also proven extremely fruitful. Glancing at the dessert menu, you see *Baudexe*, Bohemian *Buchteln*, *Kolatschen* and *Bukanzi*, *Pogatscherln* and the traitorous *Powidl*.

It can either be "a step, or a trip round the world" from Lower Austria to Vienna. In everyday conversation, the Viennese is nicknamed the "whiner". It used to be a shining metropolitan city, and now shines less, leading one quite naturally to feel more for times past than present. "A Viennese person," Hermann Bahr once said, "is a person at odds with himself, hating the Viennese, but unable to live without them."

They say that the Viennese are charming, pleasant, comfortable, tender-hearted, nice and peace-loving. Robert Schumann wrote: "I would not want to live here either for a long time or alone; here they neither seek nor understand serious people."

It can be stated as fact, or something thereabouts, that the "young" Viennese are born already "old Viennese". It is equally a fact however, that they are far from transparent. History has taught them to carry many burdens with equanimity and to take very little with total seriousness. If the Viennese become ironic, it is perhaps because they boil with anger inside, so that when they advocate their "healthy sense of humour," they may feel more like crying, when they are peaceable, they would much rather run amok, and that the legendary "Viennese golden heart" is often quite literally heavy as gold.

"Everyone that I have met up until now," Bismarck wrote in 1852, "has been extraordinarily endearing. In a business sense however, they are incredibly lazy." He was wrong on both counts, but added his weight to general Viennese stereotype. They worry little about that, in pubs singing:
"Ah am Viennese, but it ain't mah fault."

Viennese cooking, nowadays so often viewed as synonymous with Austrian cooking, is – as before mentioned – a veritable mish-mash of the recipes of a multi-racial country. To describe it roughly, one would have to say: they love clear beef soups with imaginative additions, fried things, particularly in breadcrumbs, meat roasted in its own juices without flour-based gravies, they appreciate varied desserts, prefer salad to vegetables and would find life unbearable without sweet dishes.

Burgenland did not join the Republic until 1921, and has kept "one foot in the Hungarian Pustza." The landscape, with its herds of geese, roadside villages, Magyarian houses, storks on the rooftops, wide plains and the shallow Lake Steppen, is anything other than typically Austrian. It was truly difficult for the inhabitants to become completely integrated into the Austrian family. It will take years before they can feel at home, including their cooking, in which one still finds *Halászlè* and *Haluschka*, *Fogosch* and *Tarhonya*, *Kukuruzflecken* and *Krebspörkölt*, as if it were part of Hungary.

This short perspective of the Austrian Federal States can only generalise, but makes clear nonetheless that there are wide differences between regional cooking styles and in names given to dishes. The following guide is intended not only for foreigners, but for the Austrians themselves:

Blattlen: *Blattln*, *Blattlen* or *Blattlan* in Tyrol, *Plattlan* in Carinthia, are rectangular or round pieces of dough (noodle, ground rice or potato dough), baked in the oven, or deep fried, swimming in oil.

Brein: made from millet seed and milk or water, *Brein* is one of the oldest registered foods. Still known in Burgenland, Styria and Carinthia, in more refined forms.

Buchtel: also known as *Wuchteln* or *Rohrnudeln*; or if they are very small as *Dukatenbuchteln* or *Dukatennudeln*. A sweet dish made of yeast dough. During the 19th century, a Viennese baker made *Ternobuchteln*: *Buchteln* with lottery tickets inside.

Burenhäutl: the name of the Buren sausage, a favourite take-away food.

Eierschwammerln: chantarelle mushrooms.

Einbrenn: flour, lightly browned in hot butter, used for boiled meat, vegetables or potatoes. *Einbrennte Hund* (dog) is what the Viennes call *einbrennte* potatoes.

Farferl: also *Farfel*, a soup addition, made from grated dough.

Faschiertes: meat, first minced, then mixed with a variety of ingredients to make meat balls or loaves.

Frittaten: also spelt *Fridatten*, omelettes cut like ribbon noodles, used as an addition to soups.

Gabelkraut: boiled sauerkraut, without additions.

Gansbiegel: joint of goose. A Styrian speciality, when boiled with *Ritschert*.

Golatschen: in Vienna spelt with a G, in Lower Austria with a K, a sweet dish made of yeast dough, which crossed the border from Bohemia.

Grammeln: when making bacon, suet and *Grammeln* are produced. *Grammeln* is spread on bread (*Grammelschmalz*), or made into *Grammelknödeln*, *Grammel-krapfen*, *Grammelpogatschen*, *Grammel-sterz*, *Grammelstrudel* etc. (English: greaves)

Grattler: Tyrolean potato goulash, with no meat, only smoked bacon.

G'spritzter: an eighth of a litre of wine – generally white wine – mixed with soda water.

Gupf: is a derivative of *Gugl*, *Gupf* and *Gugelhupf*, i.e. it is intended to describe something shaped into a mound. For example, a *Gupf* of whipped cream is put on a cake.

G'würznagelen: flavouring cloves.

Handgewutzelte Mohnnudeln: *wutzeln* means basically to roll. The noodles are therefore rolled by hand.

Hetschebetsch: rosehip.

Kaschernat: literally "a confusion". That is the Viennese name for a dish made with rice, paprika and tomatoes.

Katzengschroa: A type of casserole made with a variety of meats.

Koche: Viennese *Koche* in particular, made from cake, bread rolls and *Kipferln*, which is then further processed to make a dessert.

Kipfler: long, small potatoes, flavoured with a lot of bacon, which, especially in Eastern Austria, are the preference for making potato salad. A propos potatoes: In West Austria they are called *Kartoffeln*, in East Austria *Erdäpfel* (earth apples).

Kletzenbrot, Kloatzenbrot, Klotzenbrot, Kloawabrot, and **Zelten:** fruit bread would be a very general term for them all.

Krapfen: known in the Vorarl Mountains as *Krapfa*. There are *Krapfen*, sometimes made with yeast dough, at others with shortcrust pastry, and on still further occasions with

Next double page: whichever cheese the dairyman in the Bregenzer Forest churns from the milk of the lush Alm pastures, and whatever the fisherman of Lake Neusiedler finds as he empties his eel traps – the harvest is brought to the Austrian kitchen from throughout the country, and there transformed into apple strudel or Fischbeuschel soup, cheese noodles or Palffy dumplings, Schlutz-krapfen or Topfenpalatschinken.

noodle dough, using any filling imaginable. As early as in the 15th century, there were professional *Krapfen* makers in Vienna.

Krummbirn: potatoes.

Kutteln: also known as *Kuttelfleck*. In the Vorarl Mountains they are served as *saure Kuttla*. Viennese cooking knows them as *Kuttelfleck* (entrails), fried in wine sauce or in a soup.

Mus, Miasl, Muis, Muas: the West Austrian name for the East Austrian *Brein*.

Nocken: in Upper and Lower Austria they are known as *Nocken* and are more of a labourer's dish. In Salzburg they were changed into *Nockerln*, and became almost world-famous and far more refined. The Viennese changed them into *Nockerln*, in this refined form making them world famous. In Vienna, *Nockerln* were generally added to soups (*Butternockerln, millet Nockerln, liver Nockerln*), or used as a side-dish for goulash or roast meat.

Obers: whipped cream, cream.

Ochsenaug: fried egg.

Pogatscherln: are generally found in Lower Austria and are a "salted sweet dish," made with potato or yeast dough (*Kartoffelpogatscherln, Grammelpogatscherln*).

Powidltaschkerln: a Viennese song tells of them as Checkoslowakian emigrés: they are a boiled pudding, filled with plum puree.

Riebel: a type of *Schmarren*. One of the specialities of the Vorarl Mountains.

Ribisel: blackcurrants.

Ritschert: a traditional dish in Styria and Carinthia, made with beans, rolled barley and smoked meat.

Saumoasn: a Waldviertler speciality, where minced and seasoned pork is stuffed into a pig's stomach, shaped into a dumpling, boiled and then smoked.

Schmarren: dough made of a variety of ingredients, then fried and chopped: flou*r* *Schmarren*, millet *Schmarren*, bread ro*ll* *Schmarren*, potato *Schmarren*, etc.

Selchfleisch: also known as *G'selchtes* o*r* *Gsölcht's*, always meaning smoked pork.

Schlussbraten: a roasted joint of veal.

Schotten: curds, curd cheese.

Schwarzwurzen: pork smoked until its out side turns black. The fat should be ver*y* crispy and the meat dark red.

Stefaniebraten: a meat filled loaf stuffe*d* with eggs, bacon and gherkins.

Sterz: a thick porridge, made with flour maize, semolina, potatoes or beans, mashe*d* with a fork, solidified or served with variou*s* side-dishes. There are roughly a hundre*d* recipes known for this in Styria an*d* Carinthia, the most important being *Heferl sterz, Turkish Sterz* and *Mehlsterz*.

Surhaxn: knuckle of pork, marinated in salt water for between four and six weeks, the*n* oven-roasted.

Tommerl: in Styria, this sweet dish, mad*e* from a thin, fluid dough and baked wit*h* various ingredients is also called *Nigel* o*r* *Nigl*. There are apple *Tommerl*, cur*d* *Tommerl*, Turkish *Tommerl*, corn *Tommerl* or ground rice *Tommerl*.

Türteln, Tirtel, Tirschtl: pressed, round large pieces of dough, filled and deep-fried swimming in oil.

Vogerlsalat: lamb's lettuce.

Wirrler, Wirler: a type of Tyrolean potat*o* *Schmarren*.

Wefzgenescht: a fried sweet dish in th*e* shape of a wasp's nest, and almost exclusiv*e* to the Vorarl mountains.

Zwetschkenpfeffer: sauce, made with finel*y* chopped, boiled plums, steeped in spices Eaten as a puree and as a filling for noodles.

Supping Last Year's Summer Wine

We lived a life full o' pleasure
And indulged ourselves in wine
At the end of each night's endeavour
We felt like little Rothchilds fine.

It may not be totally logical, but is true nonetheless that the last of the summer wine is actually that of the previous year. Each stage is vital: first as must, then fermentation, then purification before being transferred to jugs. The whole process takes months so that only in the new year can it be called "the last of the summer wine," until the new wines of that year once again make it old.

The summer wine inns also require explanation. Originals sell only their own wine, and are open for between three weeks and six months in the year. The larger, plusher summer wine inns are generally imitations, purchasing wine from all around.

Eastern Austria is and always has been a wine producing region. Certainly as early as 400 BC the Celts were already producing wine on Austrian soil, and the Romans' long haul up the banks of the Danube was by no means necessary for the development of alcohol. However, "Good old Emperor Probus," as he is called in the Viennese songs, is with good reason often amicably regarded as the forefather of Austrian wine production. In 280 AD, it was this man who reprieved the law of Emperor Domitian which had forbidden vines to be grown outside Italy, and brought aristocratic travellers from Italy to Vienna. Under his rule, large, well organised wine plantations were constructed for the first time, appreciated above all by Roman legionaries: there was sufficient wine, and it was inexpensive, far cheaper than the precious Italian liquid once so laboriously imported.

Although the flood of pilgrims hardly felt it appropriate themselves to nurture a wine culture, the drinking tradition seems never to have ebbed away. Five hundred years after the Romans departed, there was already a plenitude of wine, as monasteries competed with each other in eagerness to plant, crusaders were far from abstemious in their bacchanal celebrations, and historians noted, not without concern, that there was much wine but few barrels. For the first time in 1300, it was necessary to build "wooden vats" to store the rich harvest. Seven hundred years ago, wine was already being produced on the banks of the Danube, in Vienna and Burgenland, with vines planted even in Salzburg.

Finding pleasure in wine, the aristocracy heavily taxed its export, forbade beer production first in Krems, then in Vienna, and while forcing out any competition, effectively stuffed their coffers with "Ungeld" – a form of ancient beverage tax.

As early as 1406 the census of the Seckau diocese registered 6000 vineyards belonging to 55 villages, and in the course of the 15th century, Vienna and Lower Austria exported roughly 100 000 hectolitres of wine each year. At the same time, Enea Silvio Piccolomini, later Pope Pius II, wrote that the Viennese wine cellars were as deep as their houses were high, while an anonymous historian passed comment that "This town, built upon barrels of wine, is a vice trap of wine, women and song."

It was then that the "Viennese and Lower Austrian buckets" were accepted throughout Austria as the new measurement, valid until 1876: 1 bucket = 40 tankards, 1 tun = 32 buckets, 1 bucket = 56.6 litres. Perusing the 1499 chronicles of wine harvest in the diocese of Melk, one finds that "A bucket of

*The gypsy who performs as part of the Last Summer Wine celebrations,
just like the young people dressed in the traditional costume of the Carinthian
Gail Valley or from Bezau in the Vorarl Mountains, the Hallstadter Knappen
brass band, the "creeping procession" in Telfs, the Rogues March in Gastein or the
Palm Sunday procession in Tyrolean Thaur – all contribute to the living customs
and customs of the Austrian countryside.*

wine was sold in the new year for two pennies. On the Southern slopes of the Vienna Forest, the same amount cost only one penny. Many people drank themselves to death." It is therefore hardly a surprise to find Emperor Maximilian trying with all his might to interest his subjects in less intoxicating passions, with puddings and pastries he had known in Burgundy. Equally unsurprising is his lack of success, and indeed, Austrian wine production enjoyed its greatest boom period at the beginning of the 16th century. In those days, the area of cultivated vineyards was ten times as large as today, with wine being produced not only in the traditional regions, but also in Upper Austria, all of Styria and Tyrol.

"Anyone caught stealing wine grapes," states a decree of the period, "shall pay for one grape with one ear, for two with both, or shall be stripped of freedom and fortune and be taken before the provincial judge."

If the Turks in 1529 had not brought discord and destruction to the idyllic Austrian vineyards with their first siege of Vienna, and if the new laws for wine production had not limited the amount of land to be cultivated, the consequences of such an uncontrolled wine flood as existed in Austria must surely have been poor quality. After this time the quality of harvests improved, and if their yield was less, there was always a sufficiency. In some areas beer was brewed once more. During the second Turkish siege of Vienna in 1683, when determined efforts were made to keep track of stores, the inventory still records 96200 hectolitres, and around the turn of the century, Abraham a Sancta Clara found it necessary to preach fire and brimstone from the pulpit: "When jugs and glasses of wine dance around the table, like the Children of Israel around the golden calf, it is then that the house will fall: our economy will recede, and poverty slither in, gold will be drunk away, leaving only copper-red noses."

According to a Royal Decree of 1784, each vineyard owner has the right to serve the wine he makes himself. Pine branches, hung over the entrance of the house, indicate that only wine made by the owner himself is served in this pub. In the small lanes of the vineyard town of Grinzing, whole rows of such "last of the summer wine" pubs can be seen.

Copper-red noses certainly seem to have been commonplace during the 18th century. In 1774 we find the decree of a Viennese Magistrate that only waiters be allowed to serve, since the countless Viennese drinking haunts were "by no means civilised, but unrestrained". The 1778 book "Viennese Anecdotes," by N. Wekherlin, advises that "If there is truth in the belief that each person, at one point in his life, must let himself go, then I strongly urge fathers send their sons to Vienna. To me this seems a place where such a spirit can be indulged but also exorcised most quickly."

Wekherlin cannot have known the summer wine pubs, since it was six years later that Emperor Josef II gave the royal dispensation for anyone "to sell and serve at any time of the year their own made food stuffs, wine and fruit cider, wherever, however and at any price they may choose." Here the chief cornerstone was laid for our present "living room inns".

As quality wine was enjoyed once more during the 18th and 19th centuries, with experiments made with Portuguese grapes and Rhine Riesling, and more and more books on wine published, the Viennese already were driving out to their cherished "living room inns," pleased as punch, in "zeiselwagens", a horse drawn cab developed by Johann Zeisel. At the end of the century came the greatest of shocks, when the terrible vine louse arrived from France, and the false malevolent flour fungus made its way into the country, probably from Italy. The vineyards were disastrously infected, the damage only somewhat allayed when the founder of the School of Wine production in Klosterneuburg succeeded in finding a prop for the European vines on vine louse resistant Californian vines.

In the last few decades, wine production has been concentrated in regions of quality yield: around Vienna, Lower Austria, Burgenland and Styria. In addition to Rhine Riesling, White Burgundy, Traminer, Welschriesling Muskat Ottonel, Müller-Thurgau, Ruhländer, early red Veltliner, Bouvier, Muska Sylvaner, Blaufränkisch, Blauer Portugieser Blue Burgundy, St. Laurent and Gelber Mus kateller a few specifically Austrian varietie can be sampled as follows:

Green Veltliner: far and away the bes known Austrian brand, drunk principally in Lower Austria and around Vienna, but also one of the most popular white wines in Burgenland. The vine prefers clay to rich soil, and only a combination of climate and soil can allow the Green Veltliner to develop its particular tangy, light and sweet taste. A favourite among wine makers because of it popularity and profitability, the wine ha been christened by them "the mortgage payer". With its pleasant acidity, it is equally popular among those frequenting the living room inns, and keeps well in storage.

Neuburger: the exact origins of the Neu burger are unknown. One can only say with certainty that it was not, as legend tells washed up from the Wachau and planted The wine has absolutely nothing in commor with flotsam and jetsam. The more recen variety, growing mainly around the Wachau near Baden, in Burgenland and around Vienna, it is a full, mild and invigorating wine, with a bouquet much loved by con noisseurs.

Zierfandler and Rotgipfler: two differen varieties, found almost exclusively in the wine-growing regions surrounding Baden They are generally marketed as a blend and are among those Gumpoldskirchner special ities that have gained excellent reputations a quality wines, far beyond their own borders The *Rotgipfler*, with its high level of citric acid, and the more heavy *Zierfandle* together make a spirited, strong and ful wine.

Schilcher: the light red Schilcher, whose name is probably derived from *schillern* (to shimmer) has been grown since the 16th

century on the prehistoric rock soil of Western Styria. It is a very particular Styrian speciality, and tastes fresh, tangy, lightly acidic and, due to its relatively high level of tannic acid, occasionally slightly bitter. Since it is produced only in a small area, this very individual wine is among the lesser-known varieties. Its followers are found mainly among those who know Styria.

Zweigeltrebe: This red wine, widely distributed throughout Lower Austria and Burgenland, is a successful new development by the director of the Klosterneuburger School of Wine Production, Dr. Fritz Zweigelt. By crossing the Blaufränkisch with the St. Laurent, he created a fine, fruity red wine, which, if stored in suitable conditions can achieve the highest quality.

Next double page: the Romans trod the grapes with their feet or their heels ("calces"), in order to squeeze out the juice ("calcare"). Also in more simple barrels than those used by the Stiftskellerei Göttweig, a clear, distinguished wine is derived from the cloudy liquid.

About Pharisäer, Einspänner
and Konsuln . . .

. . . and about *Piccolos*, *Kapuziner* and *Mazagrans*. Or to make it simpler: about coffee – second syllable accentuated with a broadly spoken e – and all the imaginative Viennese titles and means of preparing it.

In Austria, coffee is more than just a pick-me-up, since that "Turkish brew, nearly as black as ink" is the work of the coffee brewers, the coffee brewers must thank the café culture, the coffee houses are due to the literati, and the literati due to Anton Kuh, who in 1922 gave the criteria of café house authors as "somebody who has time to sit in a café and think about the things that those outside never experience."

Legend also tells that coffee was not simply a trade good that made its way from Italy to Austria, but that Kara Mustapha, when forced rather suddenly to abandon his siege of Vienna, left it in his tent. The Austrians however, glorying in victory, took these spoils of mysterious grey-green beans to be camel-fodder, a fact somewhat glossed over by later historians, who have no wish to bow to triviality and instead decided to embellish. That hot Viennese summer of 1683, as the Turks pulled their ring tighter and tighter around the city, is indeed an apt back-cloth for embellishment. The first, beautifully polished fairy-tale of the origins of Viennese coffee drinking was believed for almost three hundred years. Georg Frantzen Kolschitzky, "a Hungarian man of the town of Zombor, full of hate for all Turks, crept fearlessly through the Turkish lines on the night of the 13th August 1683, cloaked in darkness and fog," returning four days later with news of salvation, that the Emperor's reinforcement troops approached. He was awarded a multitude of the sacks in payment for this highly dangerous mission, because he had honoured

himself, and because he felt the provisions would be useful. Shortly afterwards, Kolschitzky opened up the first Viennese café house called "Beuth von Wienn".

Quite definitely – as admitted today – that is not how it was, and recent historical studies cite the first Viennese café's hour of birth as the 17th January 1685, when Emperor Leopold I granted the Armenian resident of Vienna, Johannes Diodato, the privilege of "preparing the Turkish drink as coffee, tea and sherbet."

After Diodato, the Viennese increasingly developed a taste for the honey-sweet beverage of their former worst enemies. They even allowed these barbaric arch fiends to "display their goods, build ovens and to prepare an Asian beverage, with the addition of precious water for the simple Germans. The ground Turkish drink, formerly exclusive to the coffee shops is now found roasted on coal fires on every street corner."

The rise in popularity of the new drink caused brewers of "moon-shine" to take note, and add coffee along with their fire-water to the list of "pleasure drinks". This intensely irritated the coffee brewers. By 1714 they had already requested Emperor Karl VI to grant them the clearly exclusive privilege. "Eleven citizens, their descendants, and no one else," came the order of the monarch, "shall have the right to sell or brew for sale, tea, coffee, chocolate and all varieties of sherbet."

Around 1730 there were already approximately 30 official cafés in Vienna and "a good few of the secret cellar variety." Although chocolate made an attempt in the time of Maria Theresia to oust coffee as the most popular beverage, it never really succeeded in becoming more than a coffee-

Even if the first coffee served in Vienna did not originate from the Turkish plunder of 1683, as the legend will have us believe – this magnificent Turkish tent was part of the Emperor's spoils. It is equally certain that Emperor Leopold I did, in 1685, grant the Armenian Johannes Diodato the privilege to "prepare the Turkish beverage in the form of coffee, tea and sherbet." Since then, the number of Viennese cafés has consistently increased, to the extent that Stephan Zweig claimed they were "a form of democratic club, open to everyone for the price of a cheap cup of coffee, where every member can sit for hours, discuss, write, and, above all, voraciously consume newspapers." The next double page depicts the old Café Griensteidl on St. Michaels Square.

house "tenant". And that, in spite of its vital role in the Viennese Rococo, in spite of the homage paid by Maria Theresia's own court poet Metastasio in his effusive "Cantata à la Cioccolata," and in spite of the work of court artist Liotard, who fuelled even further the smoking fires of the renowned Viennese gossip and scandal mongerers, by painting the charming Nandl Baldauf serving chocolate. The girl from the gutters fell in love with Baron Dietrichstein and the Baron was

enamoured with the chocolate-serving wench. A secret love, known to all Viennese, whose clandestine existence lasted almost a quarter of a century, before being made official on the death of the Baroness, when faithful Nandl moved to the Rococo palace.

It is unlikely that it was price that prevented chocolate surpassing coffee, even though a cup of *cioccolata* cost almost ten pennies, compared to the "thruppenny coffee". The accounts of the Berlin publisher Friedrich

Nicolai date approximately from that time, and record that "a master-tailor in Vienna will not only drink chocolate at breakfast, but it must also be the best brand." He well knew the opinion of Friedrich the Great, that "bricklayers, maids and such that work from hand to mouth should not be permitted to drink coffee," and was further incensed to note, as a citizen of his Majesty weened on beer sauce, that crowds of people inhabited the Viennese cafés and coffee gardens at all times of the day, occupied with nothing at all. Hence: "The number of people wandering from one café to the next, from one walk to the next, is really unbelievable." Indeed, although Venice can claim the accolade of inventing the café, and the Parisians and Hamburgers found pleasure in this oriental beverage somewhat before the Viennese, Vienna nonetheless quickly became a kind of breeding ground for cafés throughout Austria and the whole world. The founder of the famous Berliner Café Kranzler was the Austrian Royal Baker Johann Kranzler. In 1825 John Russell wrote that "no building in Vienna is as expensive as a café or a chemist's. This is because here, as in some other countries, nobody is permitted to follow such professions without state permission, a permission always expensive, and by no means easily obtained."

As well as coffee, chocolate, tea, almond milk, punch, lemonade and ice cream were served in the cafés, "in accordance with the seasons".

"This chap Kolschitzky," wrote a historian of the period, "who apparently still brews coffee with milk and honey, after the manner of the Turks in Schlossergasse in St. Stephan, would be astonished by the variety of concoctions a good coffee brewer already knows how to make, and by the extent of the thirst for coffee among labourers and market wenches, even though they could purchase a brew of roasted barley, sweetened with syrup at wooden stalls in the suburbs, for less than a penny."

Of course, the days of the coffee-drinkers have not all been sunny. Economic crises forced prices up, Napoleon's continental blockade made coffee scarce, and finally in 1810, sale was forbidden altogether by decree. But, as prohibitions are never entirely successful in Austria, sufficient coffee could nonetheless be obtained on payment of "a tax and 60 per cent customs charge". If the real thing was affordable, one avoided chicory, which was planted or discovered in Braunschweig in 1770, or other surrogates, like "plum stones and beech seeds." Plum stones were in any case, forbidden by decree in 1833, and only re-admitted to the market in 1836 after "carefully carried-out experiments had demonstrated that these stones, once thoroughly roasted, were not injurious to health, and hence were suitable as a basis for the preparation of coffee surrogate."

Surrogates were therefore available even after the continental blockades of Napoleon, and, if one is to believe the grumblings of contemporary moral crusaders, all coffee brewers were "avaricious swindlers". They almost certainly exaggerated however, since, when "coffee became a recipe and everyone called their own recipe what they wanted," the only concern of these vendors was to proffer their wares in unusual forms. The *Pharisäer* (Pharisee) for example, entered the annals of coffee history as a cheat and a swindler, since, although appearing as harm-

Count Dietrichstein fell in love with the chocolate serving wench Nandl Baldauf. Visitors to cafés preferred more and more the "Schogoladi". Coffee did however finally retain control. The numerous ways of preparing it demonstrate this fact (next double page).

Pharisäer

Kaffee mit Schleppe

Salon-
Einspänner

Kaffee
Maria Theresi

Einspänner

kleiner Brauner

Piccolo

Kapuziner

Capuccino

Türkischer

Kaiser-Melange

Mazagran

Konsul

großer Brauner

less coffee with cream, it certainly tastes suspiciously of rum. The *Einspänner* equally is neither a cab drawn by a single horse, nor a slice of sausage at a sausage stand, but a double mocca, served in a tall glass, topped with generous dollops of whipped cream and a sprinkling of icing sugar. Only if the whipped cream sloshes over the sides of the glass as you throw in a sugar lump, has the beverage been correctly served. By contrast, it would be a pity to spill the *Salon-Einspänner*, losing the vodka that enriches it, or the garnish of grated chocolate.

The *Konsul* again is no diplomat, but a black coffee with a splash of cream, similar to the *Piccolo* which in this case is a small black coffee with cream rather than a little bottle of champagne. Where the cream in the *Kapuziner* (Capuchin) is mixed with black coffee until assuming exactly the same colour as the Capuchin habit, the *Mazagran* is served cold, with Maraschino and ice cubes.

In addition, there is the *Kaiser-Melange* (Emperor's concoction) of egg yolk and coffee, and *Kaffee Maria Theresia* (Maria Theresia's coffee) with orange liqueur, a dollop of whipped cream, and multi-coloured sugar crystals. Etcetera, etcetera, etcetera ... The various forms of Viennese coffee would make up a small book. At least this imaginative creation of coffee variations has never been prohibited in Austria. When, in the latter half of the 19th century, sugar was planted nationally and became cheaper, it almost goes without saying that sweet puddings and coffee developed into a partnership. Most loved were those sweet dishes which perfected enjoyment of coffee without their own particular flavours intruding overly. The *Gugelhupfs* above all have had a glittering career in the realm of coffee and cakes, as have the *Strudel*, the *Kolatschen* and *Brioche*, the *Krapfen* and *Schnecken*, the *Plunderteiggebäck*, the cakes made of crumbs or biscuit dough and the *Kipferln*. Not *Kipfeln*, but *Kipferln*: *Butterkipferln*, *Briochekipferln*, *Vanillekipferln*.

In the 19th century, "fine cakes" and puddings made with "ordinary dough" became something of a prerequisite as dessert. And in the final decades they were complemented with coffee. Nowadays, this is no longer a breakfast brew, or something drunk between times in a café, but has become the final touch to any meal, in the form of a *kleiner* or *großer Brauner* (petit or grand brun), a mocca or capuccino, or as a real Turkish coffee.

Finally, an aid to those still unsure why coffee is drunk out of a nutshell or a tea cup. There are four different sizes of coffee cups: the tiny nutshell, developed at the time of the continental blockade and nowadays hardly used, the mocca cup, in which it is served "petit bruns or black," the double mocca cup, in which the Grands and doubles are made, and the teacup, used to prepare every possible concoction and mixture. Hence a "cup of coffee" can actually be a "teacup of coffee".

Given the variety of traditions, it is hardly surprising that Austrians find foreign coffee recipes and brewing methods insupportable. They are very fussy about the preparation of the brew, even regarding the water used, their own naturally the purest in the world. And, under no circumstances whatsoever would upset of their café style be tolerated, in essence very similar to the café-delicatessen. So the circle closes once more with puddings, found in a myriad of forms in the ensuing recipe section.

A Culinary Trip through Austria

After this brief survey of Austria's history and countryside, we now move to the most popular recipes, which can be found in alphabetical order, from Apple Strudel through to Wurzelkarpfen. At the end of the book, there is an index of the recipes. The ingredients throughout make up four normal portions unless otherwise indicated.

Page 50 and 51:
Austrian coffee varieties from left to right:

Pharisäer
(coffee, rum topped with cream)

Kaffee mit Schleppe
(coffee with a sweet dish)

Cappuccino

Türkischer *(Turkish)*

Einspänner
(double mocca topped with cream)

Salon-Einspänner
(double mocca, vodka topped with cream)

kleiner Brauner
(petit brun)

Kaffee Maria Theresia
(coffee, orange liqueur, sugar crystals)

Mazagran
(cold coffee on ice with Maraschino)

Kaiser-Melange
(coffee, milk, egg yolk)

Piccolo
(small black coffe with cream)

Kapuziner
(black coffee mixed with cream)

Konsul
(black coffee topped with cream)

großer Brauner *(grand brun)*

Streched Apple Strudel

The idea of wafer-thin pastry originated with the Turks. The Hungarians added apples and a certain finesse, but it was with the Viennese that this became the crowning glory of the art of cake baking. "Stretching" became a celebratory ritual. To be perfect, the pastry had to be so wafer-thin, that you could read a newspaper through it.

For the pastry:
300 g (11 oz) flour, 1 egg, 1 tablespoon oil
salt, approximately ⅛ litre luke-warm water
For the filling:
80 g (3 oz) breadcrumbs, 100 g (3½ oz) butter
1½ kg (3½ lb) thinly sliced, quite sour apples
80 g (3 oz) raisins, 100 g (3½ oz) chopped nuts
200 g (7 oz) sugar, 1 teaspoon cinnamon
½ teaspoon lemon juice

Fold together and kneed flour, oil, a pinch of salt and water to form a soft, smooth dough. Brush with a little oil, and leave to rest, covered, for 30 minutes. Then place the dough in the middle of a cloth which has been generously dusted with flour, roll it out a little, and brush again with oil. Then grasp the underside of the dough with floury hands, and draw it out carefully from the centre in all directions, until it becomes transluscent.

After cutting away any remaining thick edges of dough, fry the breadcrumbs in butter, and sprinkle them onto the dough. Mix together apples, raisins, nuts, sugar, cinnamon and lemon juice, and spread evenly over the dough.

The strudel is then rolled up by lifting the cloth. Fold over the edges, and press them closed. Roll the strudel on an oiled baking tray, brush with melted butter, and bake for 30 minutes in an oven at medium heat. Sprinkle with sugar and serve hot.

Viennese
Fried Chicken

Even in the Royal Courts – according to historians – it was common practice to pick up golden-brown chicken legs, and gnaw them with pleasure. This may be slightly lacking in style at a formal dinner, but when supping the last of the summer wine in a pub, a rural inn, or at home, it is acceptable for anyone to eat chicken with their fingers. Because chicken was among those poultry dishes reserved for the aristocracy and ruling classes according to Old Austrian law, it came to be seen as such a culinary luxury, that the populace, even when permitted, would still only treat themselves on very special occasions. Nowadays *Backhendl* are regarded as one of the most popular specialities of Viennese cooking.

2 young, tender chickens (½ chicken per person)
250 g (8½ oz) flour
2 eggs, salt
1 tablespoon oil
300 g (11 oz) breadcrumbs
oil or fat for frying
2 bunches parsley
1 lemon

Quarter and clean the chickens, turn in flour, pull through the mixture of beaten egg, salt and oil, and then press both sides into the breadcrumbs. Fry them in hot fat until they are golden-brown. Immediately after frying, let them drain on kitchen towel, then garnish with slices of lemon, and with parsley which has been pulled through the hot fat. Serve immediately.
As a side-dish serve either a green salad, or a cucumber salad prepared with sour cream, white pepper and chopped dill.

Tyrolean Farmer's Barley Broth

Barley is one of Europe's oldest cultured plants, and grows also in the alpine heights, even in the Himalayas and in Tibet. It contains primarily fibre, protein and minerals. The peeled, refined and polished barley corns – rolled or pearl barley – are particulary well suited as a basic ingredient for all broths.

A Farmer's Barley Broth such as this is a hearty dish for cold winter days, and can replace an entire meal.

150 g (5 oz) root vegetables (carrots, celeriac, parsley, leek)
1 small onion
40 g (1½ oz) butter
80 g (3 oz) pearl barley
1 joint salt pork
300 g (11 oz) bacon fat
salt
pepper
pinch nutmeg
4 strips of bacon
chives

Thinly slice root vegetables and onion, and stew in hot butter. Add pearl barley. Pour in water. Add the pork joint and bacon fat and boil slowly, until everything is well cooked and soft. Remove the meat, cube and return to the pot. Season the soup with salt, pepper and nutmeg, and serve it in an earthenware pot. Quickly fry the bacon, drape it over the soup and garnish with chives. Serve very hot. A suitable side-dish would be coarse wholemeal bread with garlic butter (salt 100 g (3½ oz) butter and mix thoroughly with 30 g (1 oz) crushed garlic).

Farmer's Mutton

In the life of every Austrian sheep, there are likely to be moments of offended vanity: on menus they are given almost inevitably the disrespectful obituary *Schöps*. At least no-one around here talks about "pulling the (sheeps) leg", but the animal that inhabits the barren mountain meadows, and not the salty lowland plains, simply cannot compete in haute cuisine with the "lamb provençale" (which despite increased sheep breeding in Austria, is still mostly imported from New Zealand). *Schöps* is simply not the most distinguished member of the sheep family. Nevertheless, the country housewife of Tyrol, Carinthia and Styria especially, understands exactly how to prepare it delightfully.

1,2 kg (2¾ lb) shoulder of mutton (Schöpsen)
salt, pepper
some flour
100 g (3½ fl oz) oil
1 large onion
1 bunch of herbs, consisting of sage, rosemary and bayleaves
1 litre red wine
2 kg (4½ lb) potatoes
100 g (3½ fl oz) oil

Cut the meat into four pieces, season with salt and pepper, dust with flour, and fry quickly in hot oil until golden-brown. In a casserole dish, briefly fry the finely chopped onion, and then add the meat and herbs. Cook everything together for a few minutes, then drown in red wine, cover, and leave to stew for roughly an hour. Peel, slice, and briefly fry the potatoes in oil, then add to the pot, and leave to stew until everything is soft.

Farmer's mutton must be served very hot, and is best brought to the table in the pan, or more stylishly in an earthenware pot. Rye bread and a strong red wine are its best accompaniments.

Pastetchen with Sweetbread Ragout

The affectionate diminuitive *Pastetchen* is typical of Viennese style. *Pastetchen* and *Pasteterln*, which are described as early as the 16th century as "made of pastry, hollow inside, and filled like a pie", are not so much eaten to combat hunger, rather as gum ticklers. For *Gusto* so to speak, as people here have named the delicate appetite always acquired by the gourmet when something exquisite is offered.

1 packet frozen puff pastry, 1 egg
For the filling:
300 g (11 oz) veal sweetbreads
salt, 50 g (2 oz) butter
40 g (1½ oz) flour
¼ litre (vealbone) stock
100 g (3½ oz) mushrooms
40 g (1½ oz) butter
freshly chopped parsley
salt, pepper
a dash lemon juice

Defrost the puff pastry. Using a pastry cutter (or two different sizes of glass), cut out four circles roughly 8 cm in diameter, and four rings of the same size (1–1½ cm thick). Place rings on top of circles, brush with beaten egg, and bake until golden brown on an oiled baking tray. Pour water over the sweetbreads, and bring slowly to the boil. Pour away the water and leave sweetbreads to cool. Blanch them in lightly salted water (boil for roughly 20 minutes), clean, and cube. Using butter and flour prepare a light gravy base, pour in the vealbone stock, and allow to boil down until it forms a creamy sauce. Gently fry mushrooms in butter, then add, with the sweetbreads, to the sauce. Flavour with parsley, salt, pepper and lemon juice. Fill the *Pastetchen* with sweetbread ragout and serve immediately.

Black Pudding Platter

The creation of black pudding is something every Austrian state would like to claim for itself, but none deserves such an accolade. The creator was a Greek named Apthonetos (alternately "the unenvied" or "the much-loved"). Peering over the shoulders of the Spartans, he watched them eat – admittedly with little relish – the black soup that their judge Lykurgos had deemed the only meal they should be permitted to eat. Apthonetos did retain pork blood in the soup, but thickened it, flavoured it with bacon and onion, stuffed it into a pig's bowel, and hence created the first black pudding.

3 black puddings
60 g (2 oz) butter or pork fat
½ kg (1 lb) of jacket boiled potatoes
60 g (2 oz) butter
1 onion
2 large sour apples

Cut black pudding into finger-thick slices, and fry well.
Peel and thinly slice potatoes. Heat butter, and fry finely chopped onion until lightly browned. Add potatoes and fry everything thoroughly. Core apples, chop into finger-thick slices, and bake in the oven until quite soft. Lay slices of black pudding on a wooden plate, garnish with apple slices, and serve with the potatoes. If desired, any remaining cooking fat can be poured over the black pudding.

Salzburg's Choux Pastry Strauben

Legend tells that the first *Straubens* were made when a love-sick cook, her head in the clouds, dropped pancake dough into hot suet. Perhaps. It is impossible to trace the path of the *Straubens* all the way to their origins, but they have certainly been made in Alpine regions for over 300 years. Perhaps this explains the manifold recipes. In Salzburg alone, there are more than half a dozen different *Strauben* doughs. The finest are those made with choux pastry.

⅛ litre milk
125 g (4½ oz) butter
pinch of salt
330 g (12 oz) flour
2 tablespoons rum
fat or oil for deep frying
50 g (2 oz) icing sugar
1 teaspoon cinnamon

Bring to the boil milk and butter with a pinch of salt. Add flour and stir until the dough becomes smooth and falls away from the sides of the pot. Allow dough to cool slightly, and then gradually fold in eggs and rum. Use a piping bag with large star nozzle to pipe *Straubens* into hot oil, and let them fry slowly, swimming in the oil. Remove the *Straubens* from the oil, and leave to drain on kitchen towel. Mix together icing sugar and cinnamon and sprinkle on the cakes.

Mixed Offal with Semolina Pancakes

Offal, or the intestines and left-overs of slaughtering, were originally something one bought directly from the slaughter-house. Nowadays, they are sold in any butcher's shop.

300 g (11 oz) onions, 120 g (4 oz) butter
300 g (11 oz) root vegetables (carrot, celeriac, parsley, leek)
1 tablespoon vinegar
1½ kg (3½ lb) offal (liver, heart, sweetbreads, spleen, breast of beef)
⅛ litre red wine
1 bayleaf, thyme, marjoram, garlic
salt, pepper, 30 g (1 oz) flour
some clear stock or water
For the semolina pancakes:
½ litre milk, 50 g (2 oz) butter
100 g (3½ oz) semolina, salt, flour, 1 egg
breadcrumbs to cover with
fat or oil for frying

Fry finely chopped onions in butter until golden yellow, then add thinly grated root vegetables and cook together for a few moments before splashing with vinegar. Then take coarsely chopped offal, excepting spleen and sweetbreads, brown all over and dowse with wine. Add herbs and leave to stew for roughly half an hour. Add to the pot strips of spleen and sliced sweetbreads, dust with flour, pour over water or clear stock, and allow everything to stew for a further 20 minutes.

Semolina pancakes: boil milk, butter, semolina and some salt until it reaches the consistency of porridge. Spread over a floured board until roughly 1½ cm thick, and leave to cool. Cut out round pancakes, turn them in flour, pull through beaten egg, press into breadcrumbs, and fry in oil until golden brown.

Tipsy Baked Apples

Just as Eve once tempted Adam, so the South Tyroleans tempt the North Tyroleans with their gorgeous apples. The red-cheeked Jonathan and the Frosted Bohemian, the shining green Golden Delicious and the Gravensteiner with its tangy aroma all came originally from one of the largest enclosed fruit farming areas in the world. But, those same items that the Tsars ordered to be brought in horse-drawn carriages, and which arrived in St Petersburg only after an exhausting trek accross half of Europe, now reach Austria in a couple of hours by train.

8 large, firm apples
100 g (3½ oz) raisins
50 g (2 oz) butter
1 tablespoon sugar
¼ litre white wine
1 pinch of cinnamon
4 tablespoons apple schnapps
Vanilla Sauce:
⅛ litre milk
1 vanilla pod
3 egg yolks
70 g (2½ oz) sugar
2 tablespoons sweet cream

Peel and core apples, fill the hollow spaces with raisins, then steam in butter, sugar and white wine, until the apples are soft and a lovely syrup has formed. Just at the end, mix in a pinch of cinnamon.

Tastefully arrange the apples on a copper tray, and pour burning apple schnapps over them.

A vanilla sauce accompanies this dish. Boil milk with vanilla pod. In a separate pot, beat together egg yolks and sugar, pour in the boiling milk, and return to the boil, stirring steadily. Strain the sauce, and garnish with a little cream.

Schönbrunn Mushrooms

The emperor Nero reputedly regarded mushrooms as a veritable food for the Gods. The only question is whether this gross garlic guzzler can be trusted to have understood the more refined, subtler taste of the mushroom. Mushrooms were nonetheless already well known in Ancient Rome. It was in the eighteenth century that they made their debut in Austrian cuisine, and, during the fever of gastronomic creation that accompanied the Vienna Congress, Schönbrunn mushrooms came into being.

500 g (1 lb) large mushrooms
salt
parsley
250 g (9 oz) chicken breast
100 g (3½ oz) ham
2 egg yolks
salt
50 g (2 oz) butter
⅛ litre sour cream
lemon juice
chives

Remove and clean mushroom stalks, chop finely, add salt, and fry with a little parsley until the juices have boiled away. Mince chicken breast and ham, bind with egg yolks, add salt, and mix thoroughly with the cooked mushroom stalks. Remove the soft interiors of the mushrooms, and pack with the prepared filling. Arrange on a buttered, ovenproof tray, and bake for half an hour in an oven pre-heated to medium temperature. From time to time, pour sour cream over the mushrooms. Before serving, sprinkle with lemon juice and chives.

Forest-Dwellers' Potato Dumplings

An epitaph for a vicar in Prinzersdorf on the Zaya, who divided his labours between the souls of his flock, and potatoes:

> To him, the planter of those roots,
> That thrive through e'en our hardest days,
> We now give thanks with joyful hoots
> To pay respect to where his soul now stays.
> So now, O traveller, doff hat and lower thine eyes
> For here's the place, where Johann Eberhard Jungblut now lies.

It was thanks to this "potato pastor", who emigrated from Holland in 1761 just after the end of the seven year war between Austria and Prussia, that these roots conquered the farm lands of lower Austria. Even today, it is in the forested areas of lower Austria that the largest potatoes are found, those the Austrians persist in calling "earth apples".

---

300 g (11 oz) boiled potatoes
1 kg (2¼ lb) raw potatoes
salt
2 tablespoons of cornflour

Peel boiled potatoes and grate finely. Grate raw potatoes into a bowl filled with cold water, then strain through a cloth, squeezing firmly. Now mix the raw and boiled potatoes, salt, and knead into a smooth dough, adding cornflour and a little of the starchy potato water as required. With wet hands, shape the dough into dumplings. Place them in boiling salty water and leave to boil vigourously for 20 minutes, and then simmer for a further 5. Dumplings are especially delicious when served with roast pork or beef.

Burgenlandian Strawberry Tart

Puddings, purees and cakes have been the much loved treats of festivals and feast days for as long as the ingredients used could set them apart from a work-a-day porridge. There are cakes for every letter of the alphabet, hundreds in total if one begins with Apple Cake and lists every variety. For each one, the season and special produce of the region play crucial roles. A Burgenlandian strawberry tart is hence no coincidence, when the most fertile strawberry plantations lie in the area surrounding Lake Neusiedler.

500 g (1 lb) strawberries
250 g (9 oz) sugar
3 egg whites
½ lemon
50 g (2 oz) butter
1 packet vanilla sugar
⅛ litre whipped cream

Wash strawberries and press through a sieve. Add sugar and mix well. Boil in a saucepan until a thick dough forms, and then leave to cool. Beat the egg whites until very stiff, and fold into the strawberry mixture along with the juice of half a lemon. Add a little grated lemon rind, and – perhaps using the lowest speed on your mixer – mix together carefully but thoroughly. Transfer the mixture to a buttered, oven proof dish and bake slowly in an oven heated to medium.
Sprinkle with vanilla sugar and serve with sweetened whipped cream. Cocktail biscuits are a particularly good accompaniment.

Esterhazian Roast Beef

"What a King can do, I can too," boasted Miklos von Esterhazy, Austrian Field Marshall and descendant of the Hungarian ruling orders, before building a Hungarian equivalent to Versailles amid the Lower Plains. Queen Maria Theresia was a guest in the magnificent castle Esterhaza; Goethe praised its luxury in "Dichtung und Wahrheit"; and Joseph Haydn spent his prime there as court director of music. It was finally a royal chef that concocted the recipe for this regally entitled roast.

4 slices of roast beef
salt, pepper
50 g (2 oz) butter or fat
250 g (9 oz) root vegetables (carrots, leek and celeriac)
1 onion, parsley
a pinch of paprika
a little flour
a little stock or water
½ lemon
⅛ litre sour cream

Salt, pepper and score the steaks, brown quickly on both sides in hot butter or oil, and then remove from the pot. Fry finely chopped onions, parsley and thinly sliced root vegetables in the remaining meat juices, flavour with paprika, dust with flour, add some stock or water and bring to the boil. Return steaks to the pot, place in the oven and leave to stew gently together until tender. At the end, flavour with lemon juice, pour in the sour cream, and bring briefly to the boil once more.
Suitable side-dishes would be Tagliatelli or noodles.

Pheasant in a Bacon Jacket

It may seem barbaric to rob the pheasant of its gloriously coloured feathers, only to stuff it inside a comparatively drab bacon jacket. The unfortunate truth is that for 1500 years now, this sacred bird from the jungles of Asia has ended its journey west inside a cooking-pot. First among the Greeks, then with the Romans, and finally by following the Roman trail, the *Avis phasionos* has made its way as a delicacy throughout all parts of the Empire. And hence to Austria, where it has principally been hunted in the meadows of the Marchfeld, near to the Hungarian border.

2 young pheasants
salt, pepper
300 g (11 oz) bacon
60 g (2 oz) butter
100 g (3½ oz) red grapes

Salt and pepper the prepared birds inside and outside. Wrap with broad, thin slices of bacon, bind like a roast chicken, and fry briefly on all sides in hot butter. Roast in an oven heated to 220–250 °C (425–475 °F) turning from time to time, and basting with its own juices, or perhaps with a little added stock. Before serving, scrape away any fat from the outside, and add the red grapes to the sauce. Suitable accompaniments would be red cabbage and croquette potatoes.

Bregenzer Whitefish Fillets

Among those fish of the powan family resembling salmon, the whitefish have become particularly popular. For centuries they have constituted the basic source of income among fishermen of Lake Constance, and are carefully categorized by them, not least for this reason. In Bregenz, whitefish are called *Heuerling* during the first stages of their lives, in the second *Stübe*, *Gangfisch* in the third, in the fourth *Renke*, in the fifth *Halbfisch* and *Dreier* in the sixth. Their season lies between May and October.

800 g (1 lb & 12 oz) whitefish fillets
salt, pepper
40 g (1½ oz) butter
1 tablespoon parsley
⅛ litre white wine
1 tablespoon lemon juice
40 g (1½ oz) butter
30 g (1 oz) flour
1 tablespoon dill
1 tablespoon whipped cream

Salt and pepper fillets and place on a buttered, ovenproof tray. Sprinkle with finely chopped parsley, dowse with wine and lemon juice, cover with tin foil and leave to stew in an oven at medium heat for 10 minutes. Arrange on a hot plate. Make a light roux with butter and flour, add fish juices and bring to the boil before adding chopped dill and whipped cream. Pour sauce over the whitefish fillets just prior to serving.
Boiled potatoes and mixed salad are suitable side dishes.

Cabbies' Gulash

Viennese cabbies are a breed apart. Since 1693 when the first professional carriage driver received his licence, the entire profession have maintained a legendary and peculiarly ritualized life-style. Even today, the few remaining horse-drawn cab drivers sport the traditional attire: checked trousers, a velvet jacket, and a stiff hat, called a *Stößer*. The gulash bearing their name has equally idiosyncratic decoration, hiding Hungarian origins under a Viennese cloak.

1 kg (2¼ lb) joint of beef
100 g (3½ oz) pork fat
800 g (1 lb & 12 oz) onions
a splash vinegar
40 g (1½ oz) paprika (mild)
1 tablespoon tomato puree
1 clove garlic
a little marjoram
caraway
salt
4 eggs
2 pairs frankfurter sausages
4 pickled gherkins

Cube the meat or cut into coarse slices. Fry chopped onions in hot fat until golden brown, then splash with some vinegary water. Add meat, paprika, tomato puree, crushed garlic, marjoram, caraway and salt, and leave to boil first of all in its own juices. As soon as these have evaporated, replace with a little water, repeating this process at intervals while the meat stews. Once the meat is tender, pour in enough water so that it is just covered by sauce. Leave to stew for a further 10 minutes until red-brown globules of fat form on the surface. To add a certain style, serve cabbies' gulash in individual copper bowls, garnished with a fried egg, a single frankfurter, and a gherkin sliced into the shape of a fan.

Fish Soup

A true Danube speciality, the supping of which apparently prompted Johann Nestroy to state: "If they fished an old boot out of the river, these Viennese gourmets would concoct such an exquisite little soup from it, that the same Venus who is said to have created the Bouillabaisse, would turn green with envy."

A carp's head, tail and bones
1 onion
a small bayleaf
peppercorns, thyme
2 tablespoons vinegar, salt
carp's roe
a splash of vinegar, salt
1 teaspoon sugar
50 g (2 oz) butter
40 g (1½ oz) flour
120 g (4 oz) root vegetables (carrot, parsley, celeriac, leek)
⅛ litre red wine
4 tablespoons sour cream
lemon juice
parsley
cubes of white bread

Thoroughly wash carp's head, tail and bones, and place in approximately 1½ litre water, with onion, bayleaf, peppercorns, thyme, vinegar and salt, and boil slowly until soft. Strip flesh from the bones, chop roughly, and keep warm. In a second pot, boil carp in a little water with vinegar, salt and sugar, then mash with a fork, and whisk together.
In a third pot, make a simple roux of butter and flour, fry grated root vegetables briefly, then dowse with red wine. Carefully strain the fish stock, pour it over the root vegetables and boil again for 15 minutes. Finally, add fish and roe, flavouring the soup with sour cream and lemon juice.
Serve the soup garnished with chopped parsley and white bread croutons.

Leg of Chamois Goat

The supper-time guests you cannot invite,
Until you've caught a goat for the night.

The chamois goat lives in herds on the
Alpine slopes, eking out an existence on
herbs and bushes. Maximilian I was in-
trigued by this animal, so shy and elusive,
and invented a special goat hunt without
crossbow or shotgun. The animals were
driven across difficult terrain, then lanced by
bold hunters carrying long spears.

Sauce:
½ litre red wine
½ litre water
300 g (11 oz) root vegetables (carrots, cele-
riac, parsley)
1 onion, 1 bayleaf, peppercorns, sage
For the roast:
1 goat's leg, 150 g (5 oz) bacon
60 g (2 oz) butter, 30 g (1 oz) flour

At the start, boil together all the sauce ingredients, then set aside to cool. Layer some
of the sliced root vegetables on the base of a
china or earthenware pot. Discarding skin
and bones, arrange the meat on top of this
vegetable layer and then cover with a further
layer of vegetables. Pour the sauce over,
completely covering the meat. Fit the lid
securely, and leave in a cool place for between three and five days. After this time,
remove the meat and press dry. Wrap in
bacon, and, using a casserole dish, fry
thoroughly on all sides in butter and bacon
fat. Dowse with the sauce, adding approximately half the root vegetables, and then
stew until soft. Strain sauce, thicken with a
little flour. When very hot, pour over the
sliced meat.
An ideal accompaniment would be bread
dumplings and chantarelle mushrooms, with
a garnish of orange baskets filled with cranberries.

Burgenländer Goose Liver

Sunshine soaked village streets, white poultry calmly waddling across the road: Burgenland. Terrified drivers will testify to this, and with considerably less enthusiasm than the gourmets. To a goose however, it makes little difference in the end, and especially to the Burgenland geese, whose reputation for excellent meat and lovely, plump white livers has for centuries led them straight into the cooking pot.

---

400 g (14 oz) goose liver
½ litre milk
salt
100 g (3½ oz) goose fat
1 small onion
a pinch of paprika

Wash goose liver thoroughly, and leave to rest in milk for half an hour. Remove, dry and salt it. Heat fat in a casserole dish, add chopped onions and complete liver, and roast in a pre-heated oven for half an hour, basting with water several times. Slice the liver, arrange on a pre-heated serving dish, mix meat juices and paprika, and pour over. Serve very hot. Slices of baked apple and toast accompany this dish very well.

Yeasty Dumplings with Grated Poppy Seeds

The poppy, which is indigenous to Asia, was already current among Stone Age farmers. Equally, the medicinal qualities of yeast were known to Ancient Greeks and Babylonians. No-one can say at exactly which time yeast, poppy seeds and plum jam were first combined by Austrian chefs. All that can be said is that Queen Maria Theresia gave instructions for plum jam to be specially imported by the barrel-load from Prague.

250 g (9 oz) flour
4 tablespoons milk
10 g (⅓ oz) yeast, 10 g (⅓ oz) sugar, salt
1 egg yolk
30 g (1 oz) butter, a little milk
100 g (3½ oz) plum jam
1 teaspoon rum, pinch cinnamon
50 g (2 oz) grated poppy seeds
60 g (2 oz) icing sugar
60 g (2 oz) butter

Put flour into a large bowl. Warm the milk a little, then stir in the crumbled yeast and sugar until smooth, and pour over the flour. Add to this salt, egg yolk and melted butter, and knead to a smooth dough – perhaps adding a little milk – then beat with a wooden spoon until the dough falls easily away. Cover with a cloth, and leave in a warm place for approximately one hour.

Thoroughly mix plum jam, rum and cinnamon. Divide risen dough into twelve equal portions, insert a teaspoon of plum jam into the centre of each one, flatten slightly and shape into dumplings. Arrange on a floured baking tray, and leave to rise for a further 25 minutes. Then, simmer in slightly salted water for 6 minutes, turn, and leave to boil for a further 6 minutes.

Serve sprinkled generously with sugar and poppy seeds, and pour melted butter over.

Roast of Vorarl Mountain Goat

In the Vorarl mountains, young goats have the name *Gitzis*, and in the rest of Austria, *Kitz*. Young kid goats are particular favourite as a dish for Easter and were at one time always prepared over the kitchen fire. Nowadays we tend to put them in the oven, but the seasoning remains the same. Now as then, the aroma of the roast goat must be dominated by marjoram.

In Austria, the best marjoram comes from the Burgenland. The so-called Neusiedler marjoram is planted in spring among the salad vegetables, and tended according to time honoured methods, passed down through many generations.

1½ kg (3½ lb) kid goat
salt, pepper
½ teaspoon marjoram
500 g (1 lb) potatoes

Salt and pepper the meat, rub well with marjoram, and fry on all sides in butter. Cover with thin slices of butter, place in the oven and roast at a medium temperature. After roughly half an hour, add small, peeled, whole potatoes, salt, and leave to roast further, until the meat and the potatoes are soft. Serve the roast goat with a green salad.

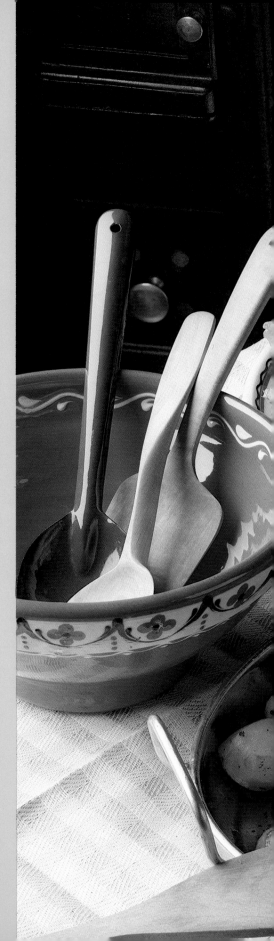

Semolina Noodles with Mulled Wine

The same cinnamon that is such an essential ingredient of mulled wine, can be found in a Chinese cookery book dating back 2800 years before the birth of Christ. It took 3000 years for this dried interior of the cinnamon tree's bark to reach Austrian shores for the first time. As the story goes, a Roman Centurian watched his men loose heart trying to build a road over the Tauern Pass amid high winds and blizzards, and instructed that copious quantities of wine be brewed with generous additions of cinnamon. His treatment must have taken effect, since the road was completed.

½ litre milk, salt, 120 g (4 oz) semolina
50 g (2 oz) butter, 1 egg yolk, lemon rind
100 g (3½ oz) flour, 2 eggs
150 g (5 oz) breadcrumbs, oil for frying
Mulled wine:
1 litre red wine
100 g (3½ oz)–200 g (7 oz) sugar (according to taste), 10 cloves
2 cinnamon sticks, the length of your little finger
1 slice lemon

Boil milk with a little salt, stir in the semolina and leave to simmer for a few minutes. In a bowl, beat butter until creamy, add egg yolk, a little lemon rind, and stir in the boiled semolina to form a loose dough. Make noodles from the dough, roll in flour, dip in beaten egg, and press into breadcrumbs. Heat oil, and fry the noodles until golden-brown.
Mulled wine: Heat red wine (diluted with some water as desired) and all other ingredients in a glazed pot, bring almost to the boil, and serve immediately.
Pour some of the mulled wine like a sauce over the dumplings, serving the rest in mugs.

Tyrolean Gröstl

"Every inn," reported August von Kotzebue after his 1804 journey through Tyrol, "serves a gentleman's supper, a coachman's supper and wedding supper, the last of which costs a woman eight pence less than it costs a man".

Today one can still find a Man's Platter and a Farmer's Platter, but it is the latter of these that is equivalent to the true, the original Tyrolean *Gröstl*.

60 g (2 oz) butter (or pork fat)
1 onion
500 g (1 lb) boiled beef
150 g (5 oz) smoked sausage
salt, pepper
marjoram
500 g (1 lb) boiled potatoes
50 g (2 oz) butter
salt
parsley

Fry finely chopped onions in hot butter until golden-brown, add thinly sliced meat and sausage, season with salt, pepper and a little marjoram, and fry together for a few minutes.

Peel and thinly slice potatoes. In a second pan, fry in hot butter until slightly crispy, salt, mix with the meat, and sprinkle with chopped parsley.

Coleslaw or a bacon sauerkraut should be served with *Gröstl* or Tyrolean *Gröschtl*.

Bacon sauerkraut: steam 500 g (1 lb) sauerkraut until soft. Fry 150 g (5 oz) of cubed bacon with onions. Mix together, season with salt and caraway, and leave to steam again briefly together.

Pike in Anchovy Sauce

Pike is the rogue of the sweet waters. Fish, frogs and small water birds all fall prey to the sharp teeth and insatiable appetite of an animal that does not even stop short when it comes to his own kith and kin. Studies have demonstrated that 97 per cent of all young pike are devoured by their own relatives. At the age of two however, the rogue himself is ripe for the pot. At this age they weigh between two and three kilogrammes, and their fillets in particular are succulent and tender.

4 pike fillets
salt, pepper
lemon juice
50 g (2 oz) butter
4 anchovies
parsley
2 tablespoons beef stock

Rub pike fillets with salt, pepper and lemon juice, then fry slowly in butter until both sides are golden-brown. Remove from the pan, and arrange on a pre-heated serving dish. Finely chop anchovies and parsley, add to the frying juices, and bring to the boil with some beef stock before pouring over the fillets.
The dish is at its best served with bouillon potatoes: peel small, raw potatoes, and boil in beef stock with sliced root vegetables until soft. Strain and discard stock, and serve potatoes together with the vegetables.

Brain Pofesen

Opinions differ regarding *Pofesen*: some call them *Bofesen*, and claim Maria Theresia's personal chef as their inventor; others make a plea for *Bovesen*; in some valleys they are *Profesen*; and finally *Pavesen* may also be heard, since they are made with bread like the *Zuppa Pavese* and are occasionally shaped into the emblem of the *Pavese*, the inhabitants of Pavia in the Middle Ages. The spelling *Pofesen* is essentially a compromise, and as such, typically Austrian.

500 g (1 lb) veal brain
50 g (2 oz) butter
½ onion
1 egg yolk
parsley
salt, pepper
lemon juice
8 slices white bread (square toasting bread)
⅛ litre milk
2 eggs
150 g (5 oz) breadcrumbs
oil for frying

Plunge veal brain in hot water, then skin and finely chop. Fry finely chopped onion in butter until brown, add brain and continue frying until cooked through. Remove from heat, bind with egg yolk and season with chopped parsley, salt, pepper and lemon juice.
In between times, pull bread slices through a mixture of beaten eggs and milk, turn in breadcrumbs and fry in oil until yellow-golden.
Spread the brain mixture on one piece of fried bread, and cover with the second slice. It is possible to do this before frying the bread, but spreading later avoids the Povesen falling apart when frying.
Serve with a side-dish of green salad.

Montafoner Venison

The valley of the River Ill that lies between Ratikon's peak and the Verwall group, is famed for its tasty game dishes. Even on the table, Montafoner venison remains surrounded by everything indigenous to its natural habitat: by juniper berries, with their bitter-sweet, resiny taste; by chantarelle mushrooms, always slightly reminiscent of the forest; and by tangy-sweet cranberries.

1 venison back
salt, pepper
100 g (3½ oz) bacon
60 g (2 oz) butter
juniper berries
40 g (1½ oz) butter
1 tablespoon chopped parsley
300 g (11 oz) chantarelle mushrooms

Rub a well hung venison back with salt and pepper, and cover evenly with strips of bacon. Lay in a roasting tray, meat side down, add juniper berries, and pour over melted butter. Roast at medium temperature, basting repeatedly with butter from the pan, and as soon as the meat is tender, turn and continue roasting until cooked through, if necessary basting with a little stock.
Heat butter in a second casserole dish and briefly fry finely chopped parsley. Add whole – or coarsley chopped – young chantarelle mushrooms, and fry. Lay venison on a pre-heated serving dish, garnish with the chantarelle mushrooms, and serve with noodles and cranberries.

Ancient Viennese Chicken Broth

An appreciation of chicken broth and egg dishes is a legacy of our predecessors. Hence, a recipe for chicken broth, then prepared with chicken and rabbit, blood and herbs, can be found dating back to the 15th century.

1 small chicken
150 g (5 oz) root vegetables (carrots, celeriac, leek, parsley)
150 g (5 oz) mushrooms
100 g (3½ oz) peas
salt, nutmeg
Marrow dumplings:
2 bread rolls
1 egg
50 g (2 oz) beef marrow
parsley, salt, breadcrumbs

Place the gutted chicken, along with heart, intestines and liver in 2½ litres of cold water, bring to the boil, spoon off the foam, add root vegetables, and boil slowly until tender.

In a saucepan, steam finely chopped root vegetables, mushrooms and the peas with a little stock, and as soon as everything is cooked through, add to the soup.

Take the boiled chicken out of its stock, strip meat from the bones, cut into strips, and place in a soup bowl, together with finely sliced intestines. Season the soup with salt and a little nutmeg, then pour, together with the boiled vegetables, over the chicken.

Marrow dumplings should be prepared beforehand: soften bread rolls in a little water, squeeze, discarding excess water, mix together with egg and soft beef marrow, add a little chopped parsley, and bind with the breadcrumbs. Form small dumplings. Boil in salty water for 8 minutes, and place in the soup.

Netted Hunter's Roast

Don't be put off by the name. Here, "hunter" does not represent trapped game, rather the forest, and forest mushrooms, and equally the net has not been stolen from a fisherman, but from a pig.

1 onion
50 g (2 oz) butter
1 bread roll
⅛ litre milk
500 g (1 lb) mixed minced beef and pork
1 egg
salt, pepper
parsley
1 pig's caul
40 g (1½ oz) butter
200 g (7 oz) mushrooms
⅛ litre sour cream

Fry finely chopped onions in butter until golden-brown. Soften bread rolls in milk. Knead minced meat together with fried onions, softened bread rolls, egg, salt, pepper and chopped parsley to form a smooth dough. With wet hands, roll the mixture into a cylinder, and slip into the pig's caul. Lay the roll on a buttered baking tray, and roast in the oven at medium temperature, basting regularly. A suitable accompaniment would be polenta.

Styrian Hunter's Loaf

You don't have to be a hunter to take to the mountains, and to enjoy Hunter's Loaf, you needn't first carry it arround in a ruck-sack. Indeed, it is equally suitable as a provision for your guests, and has the added advantage of remaining perfectly fresh for two or three days, wrapped in foil in the fridge.

1 loaf white bread
100 g (3½ oz) butter
2 anchovies
2 hard boiled eggs
parsley
1 tablespoon oil
salt, pepper
100 g (3½ oz) ham
100 g (3½ oz) tongue
100 g (3½ oz) salami
100 g (3½ oz) edam cheese
100 g (3½ oz) sausage
2 pickled gherkins
10 pistacio nuts

To prepare the loaf, cut off each end and use the handle of a cooking spoon to hollow it out, until the crust, and roughly 1 cm of bread remain.
Beat butter until creamy, strain anchovies and separate yolk from egg, finely chop parsley, and mix well with oil, salt and pepper. Chop remaining ingredients into small cubes, and add to the mixture. Stuff this filling into the hollowed out loaf, leaving no spaces. Replace the ends of the bread, wrap in greaseproof paper or aluminium foil, and place in the fridge. After one hour it is ready. Cut into 1 cm thick slices, and arrange nicely before serving.

The Emperor's Gugelhupf Cake

"Perhaps I could tempt his Majesty to a slice of Gugelhupf," were the words of court actress Katharina Schratt, baker's daughter and wife of the careless and heavily indebted Hungarian Baron Kiß von Itepe, to the Emperor Franz Joseph. Or at least, so the story goes. Franz Joseph accepted her offer, and one *Gugelhupf* grew into a series of *Gugelhupfs*. Even now, this greatest of all breakfast dishes continues to provide authors with considerable material for legends.

¼ litre milk
30 g (1 oz) yeast
1 tablespoon flour
150 g (5 oz) butter
100 g (3½ oz) sugar
8 egg yolks
80 g (3½ oz) raisins
a pinch of salt, lemon peel
500 g (1 lb) flour
100 g (3½ oz) sliced almonds
icing sugar

Make a so-called *Dampferl* (a bit of smooth dough) with luke-warm milk, yeast and 1 tablespoon flour. Place in a warm place and leave to rise until the mixture has doubled in size. Beat butter and sugar until creamy. Gradually add egg yolk, raisins, a pinch of salt, grated lemon peel and flour. Mix with the dough until smooth, then beat until it separates from the spoon, and appears almost "silky". Empty into a high, buttered cake mould, and sprinkle with chopped almonds. Cover and leave in a warm place until the dough has risen again to the edges of the mould. Then bake at medium temperature for 40 minutes. Knock the cake out of its mould onto a board, allow to cool, and serve sprinkled with icing sugar.

The Emperor's Scraps

Schmarren was the child of a humble farmer's kitchen, whose career has prospered through the passing centuries. Originally prepared with ground semolina and either water or milk, it was not until much, much later that it came into contact with sugar and raisins. In all probability it never met the Emperor. A folklore tale of the Emperor getting lost while hunting, and startling a farmer's wife to such a degree that her omelette fell into *Schmarren*, is, after all, pure legend.

200 g (7 oz) flour
pinch salt
4 egg yolks
¼ litre milk
4 egg whites
30 g (1 oz) icing sugar
a little butter
40 g (1½ oz) raisins
butter for frying
icing sugar

Fold together flour, salt, egg yolks and milk to a smooth batter, then mix carefully with egg whites and the sugar, which have been whipped until creamy and stiff. Heat butter in a frying pan, then pour in the dough to form a finger-thick layer, and sprinkle raisins over it. As soon as the underside of the dough is golden-brown, turn, and fry on the other side. Using a fork, cut the dough into small pieces, and arrange on a serving plate, sprinkle with icing sugar, and serve straight away. Slightly bitter cranberry sauce makes a particularly suitable accompaniment.

The Emperor's Schnitzel

The list of Austria's schnitzels is almost end-less: Wiener Schnitzel, Nature's Schnitzel, Sardine Schnitzel, Pepper Schnitzel, Mushroom Schnitzel, Gypsy Schnitzel, Parmesan Schnitzel, Cream Schnitzel etc. One of our most ancient recipes is used to make the Emperor's Schnitzel.

4 veal joint schnitzels
salt
30 g (1 oz) flour
40 g (1½ oz) butter
½ onion
lemon peel
1 tablespoon capers
1 teaspoon chopped parsley
a little flour
⅛ litre white wine
⅛ litre sour cream
⅛ meat stock

Pound the veal schnitzels, and slightly score the edges, so that they don't roll up. Salt, and rub one side in flour. Heat butter, and fry first on the floured side. As soon as it is golden-brown, turn, and fry on the other side. Remove schnitzels from the pan and keep warm. Fry finely chopped onion half in the remaining meat juices with a little grated lemon rind, then add capers and parsley, dust with some flour, dowse with wine and sour cream, and allow to simmer gently before boiling down with the meat stock to form a thick sauce. Pour sauce over the schnitzels. Suitable side dishes are rice and fresh green salad.

Fried Veal Sweetbread

Three hundred years ago, in the kitchen of Salzburg's archbishop, at least a dozen gourmet recipes were already being used to cook sweetbread. In those days it was either prepared very elaborately, with mussels and morels, or used as an accompaniment to other meat dishes. Today the sweetbread's own fine, delicate taste is treated with greater respect, instead of swamping it with too many other flavours.

500 g (1 lb) veal sweetbreads
salt
100 g (3½ oz) flour
2 eggs
2 tablespoons milk
100 g (3½ oz) breadcrumbs
oil for frying
1 lemon

Thoroughly wash sweetbreads in cold water, bring to the boil, and, after allowing to cool down, wash again. Cut into finger-thick slices, salt, turn in flour, dip into a mixture of beaten eggs and milk, then press into breadcrumbs. Fry on both sides, swimming in a lot of oil, until golden brown. Serve garnished with slices of lemon. A suitable side dish for fried sweetbread would be green salad.

Veal Kidney with Saffron Rice

Saffron is derived from a red-yellow coloured substance found in the calyx of a bright violet blooming crocus. It is the most valuable spice in the world. For a single kilogramme of saffron, 100 000 plants must be harvested. One of the best forms of saffron comes from the Cashmere region in India, but it can also be gleaned from Austrian crocus plants. And, saffron cakes are not the only thing it can be used for. In the last century, it made it's way into soups, from there to the *Risotto Milanese*, and hence into a variety of rice dishes, particularly in Tyrol and Carinthia.

2 tablespoons oil
1 small onion
350 g (12 oz) rice
beef stock
½ teaspoon saffron
2 veal kidneys
salt, pepper, 2 tablespoons oil

Heat oil in a saucepan, and lightly brown finely chopped onions. Add dry rice and stir until it is transluscent. Dowse with some stock. Pour in saffron, dissolved in hot water, add salt, and boil rice slowly over a low heat, occasionally adding stock (in total not more than 1½ litre), and stirring continuously. Stop stirring only when very little of the liquid is left and the rice is ready. As soon as the consistency of the mixture is thick enough, remove from the heat, and leave aside to rest for a little while.

Remove some of the fat from around the kidneys, wash in cold running water, add salt, pepper, cut into finger-thick slices, brush on both sides with oil, and place under a pre-heated grill.

As soon as the kidneys are cooked through, serve on saffron rice with a green salad.

Old Tyrolean Capucin Roast

There is only a figurative connection between this dish and the Capucin Order. Slices of kidney make a kind of hood or cowl for the veal, and, even as the cowl on the robes of the monks lent its name to their order, so the same name is lent by the meat's decoration.

4 slices veal
4 slices veal kidneys
salt, pepper
2 tablespoons oil
⅛ litre white wine
200 g (7 oz) boiled green beans
4 slices smoked bacon
1 small clove of garlic
basil

Remove fat from around the kidneys, and, using a toothpick, attach one piece to each slice of veal, then season with salt and pepper, brush generously with oil, and fry quickly on both sides. Place in a saucepan with a little oil and white wine. Add boiled beans and slices of bacon, flavoured with garlic and basil, and stew slowly together until cooked through. Serve the Capucin Roast very hot, with a dish of chive potatoes at the side.

Carinthian Stuffed Noodles

In the Middle Ages they were called stuffed pasties, which is actually more correct, since although this Carinthian national dish is made with noodle dough, it bears no resemblance to true noodles. The distinctive feature of the stuffed noodles is not so much their shape, as their filling. They originate from an age when the production of milk and cheese was one of the chief sources of income for the Carinthian populace.

500 g (1 lb) flour
1 egg
salt, 1 tablespoon oil
water
Filling: 500 g (1 lb) dry curd cheese
250 g (9 oz) boiled, strained potatoes
2 eggs
salt, mint, chives
sour cream as necessary
100 g (3½ oz) butter
parsley

Prepare a smooth, silky noodle dough from flour, egg, salt and water, and leave to rest for a while. In the meantime, thoroughly mix together the filling ingredients, if necessary, thinning with a little sour cream.
Roll out dough on a floury board until a few millimeters thick. Cut out circles, 8–10 cm in diameter, place a tablespoon of filling on each one, fold over, and press the sides together very firmly. Place the noodles, which now look like small pasties, in salted boiling water, and boil for 10–12 minutes. As they rise to the surface, remove, and leave to drain thoroughly, before arranging on a serving dish, pouring melted butter over them, and garnishing with a little chopped parsley.
A Carinthian fruit schnapps should not be omitted from a meal of stuffed noodles.

Chestnut Cream Whip

Just for a moment, forget the calories: this is no dish for slimmers! The chestnut, originally of the Kastana territory in Asia Minor, first made its way into Europe via Sicily, and from there travelled North. In Austria they gained currency towards the middle of the eighteenth century, and were quickly combined with the then inexpensive beet sugar. It was in 1799 that Baron von Jaquin cultivated the first mangel wurzels in the Vienna Botanical Gardens, and it didn't take long for this inexpensive beet sugar to supersede the refined cane product, clearing the path for creation of Austrian cream desserts.

½ kg (1 lb) chestnuts
150 g (5 oz) sugar
1 packet vanilla sugar
2 tablespoons Maraschino
½ litre whipping cream
20 g (½ oz) icing sugar
glacé cherries

Peel chestnuts, boil and strain. Allow mixture to cool, then stir in sugar, vanilla sugar and Maraschino. Whip cream with icing sugar until very stiff, and fold carefully into the chestnut puree. Fill goblet bowls with the mixture, chill, and garnish with a glacé cherry.

Styrian Knuckle of Pork

Stryria, first to join the Austrian union, and its capital city Graz, also capital city of inner Austria for several decades during the sixteenth and seventeenth centuries, is regarded – next to Tyrol – as the epicentre of recipe-writing. In 1607, following the order of one man, Styrian Baron Max, six hundred recipes were transcribed by hand, and in 1686, the first print-run of a cookery book took place in Graz. These early books were however, only for use within courtly kitchens. Only in the last years of the eighteenth century was a Grazian cookery book published which catered for the man on the street.

1 pork knuckle
150 g (5 oz) root vegetables
salt
1 bayleaf
juniper berries and peppercorns
marjoram
40 g (1½ oz) butter
40 g (1½ oz) flour
1 tablespoon vinegar
cubed white bread
chives

Ask the butcher to saw the pork knuckle into roughly 2 cm thick slices. Boil in water with root vegetables and herbs until tender. Use melted butter and flour to make a light roux. Pour in strained stock and flavour with a splash of vinegar. Fry white breadcrumbs in butter until golden brown, then sprinkle over the soup with finely chopped parsley. Serve the pork knuckle slices with boiled, salted potatoes and freshly grated horseradish.

Tyrolean Pastries

In days gone bye, turnovers were made in farm kitchens, and there served with a sweet dripping of milk, flour, sugar, butter and honey. Nowadays, a glance at the calorie counter suggests we should steer away from the sweet dripping, and concentrate instead on the quality of the filling. Even here however, the relatively rich concoction of dried pears, figs, poppy seeds and breadcrumbs has generally been surplanted by jam. I would suggest the use of a raspberry or cranberry conserve.

⅛ litre milk
120 g (4 oz) butter
500 g (1 lb) flour
pinch salt
200 g (7 oz) jam
50 g (2 oz) breadcrumbs
oil or fat for baking

Heat milk and let butter melt in it slowly. Heap flour on a board, salt, and knead into quite a firm dough with the butter-milk mixture. Leave the dough to rest for approximately ½ hour. Roll out thinly, and cut into squares approximately 12 cm in size. Place a tablespoon of jam, mixed with breadcrumbs in the centre of each square, fold them over to form triangles, then roll the edges into bows using a rolling pin. Press the edges firmly together.

Bake the pastries in a generous amount of oil and then leave to drain on kitchen towel. Arrange on a wooden board, and, if possible, serve straight away. If this is not possible, cover with a linen napkin, and keep warm in the oven at 50 °C (120 °F), leaving the oven doors open.

Tyrolean Liver with Polenta

Viennese cuisine has never really been sure how to deal with polenta. Originally cooked by apprentice woodcutters in a *Plentn* cauldron over an open wood fire, the dish has remained an Alpine speciality: in Tyrol it is known as *Polenta* or *Plentn*; in Carinthia and Styria as Turkish *Stertz*; and in Salzburg as *Plentenkoch*. Even today the enthusiast will claim polenta cooked in a copper pot to be unsurpassable. All the same, use a conventional pot, serve with liver, gulash, *Beuschel*, kidney or game, add a strong gravy, and the tastiness of the dish is unquestionable.

500 g (1 lb) veal liver
100 g (3½ oz) bacon
1 onion
40 g (1½ oz) butter
1 tablespoon flour
salt, pepper
lemon juice, capers
⅛ l white wine
⅛ l beef stock
For the polenta:
300 g (11 oz) cornmeal
approx. 1½ litre water, salt
50 g (2 oz) butter

Thinly slice liver, and fry first of all with slices of bacon and chopped onion, then dust with flour and fry thoroughly, seasoned with salt, pepper, lemon juice and capers. Dowse with wine and beef stock, and leave to simmer.
Polenta: Pour the cornmeal into salted boiling water, stirring constantly. Boil for approximately 30 minutes, still stirring, until the polenta separates from the sides of the pot. Press the mixture into a mould which has been splashed with water, then turn out onto a board. Top with some butter slices, and serve straight away.

Linzer Torte

The city of Linz was not in fact mother to Linzer Torte, a far more likely candidate being the courtly kitchens of the Salzburg archbishops at the turn of the eighteenth century. Indeed, it was not even a Linzer who brought the torte to fame, but the traveller, Count Hermann von Pückler-Muskau, himself famed less for his travel and horticultural writings than for his eccentricity and enjoyment of fine desserts.

140 g (5 oz) flour
140 g (5 oz) butter
140 g (5 oz) ground almonds
140 g (5 oz) sugar
1 egg
½ teaspoon cinnamon
pinch of ground cloves
½ lemon
1 coffee cup blackcurrant jam
1 beaten egg
40 g (1½ oz) chopped almonds
1 packet vanilla sugar, icing sugar

Heap flour on a board and rub together with butter, then knead into a smooth dough with almonds, sugar, egg, cinnamon, ground cloves and the juice of half a lemon. Divide the finished dough in two and leave to rest for approximately half and hour. Brush a tart tray with melted butter, and, using your hands, press one half of the dough into it. Spread blackcurrant jam over this. Roll out the other half of the dough, and cut strips approximately 1½ cm in width, then lay these over the jam in a lattice pattern. Brush the lattice with beaten egg and sprinkle with chopped almonds. Bake the tart in an oven at medium temperature for approximately an hour, or until golden brown. Mix vanilla sugar and icing sugar, and sprinkle over the tart.

Linzer Torte can be stored after baking. Even days later, it still tastes fresh.

Liptauer Cheese

As far as it is possible to establish the origins of the *Liptauer*, it seems that butter was first stirred into sheep's curd cheese and coloured with a pinch of paprika over one hundred years ago, by a Transylvanian housewife. It is therefore a moot point whether the *Liptauer* is a Hungarian, Austrian, or – as the culinary xenophobe might claim – a Bohemian speciality. One thing only is certain: that Austrian cuisine could no longer do witout this spicy cream cheese.

200 g (7 oz) curd cheese
200 g (7 oz) butter
1 small onion
2 tablespoons sour cream
1 teaspoon mustard
8–10 chopped capers
1 puréed anchovy
1 gherkin
caraway, salt, pepper
1 teaspoon mild paprika

Strain curd cheese, beat butter until creamy, and mix. Stir in finely chopped onion, sour cream, mustard, capers, anchovy and finely chopped gherkin, season with caraway, salt, pepper and paprika, and mix thoroughly. Liptauer is served with radishes, salt pretzels and strips of green pepper.
To create a pleasing visual effect, pack Liptauer into a hollowed out green pepper, leave in the fridge for a couple of hours, then cut into slices of approximately ½ cm thickness. These Liptauer rings are particularly suitable as a garnish for cheese platters.

Wachauer Apricot Dumplings

Where would Wachauer cuisine be without the richly aromatic, juicy, tasty apricots? The famous Wachauer apricot gardens begin near Aggbach, directly underneath the Raubritterhorst Aggstein, and, on the other Danube bank, underneath the legendary Tausendeimer Mountain, you will find the unrivalled apricot capital, Spitz. Here they celebrate a fete day for the fruit, and this is where the best apricot dumplings are made, according to the oldest of recipes.

1 kg (2¼ lb) potatoes
350 g (12 oz) flour
40 g (1½ oz) butter
1 egg
pinch salt
500 g (1 lb) apricots
sugar cubes
4 tablespoons apricot liqueur
80 g (3 oz) butter
100 g (3½ oz) breadcrumbs
icing sugar

Boil potatoes in their skins until soft, then strain and peel. While they are still warm, knead to a smooth dough with flour, butter, egg and salt. Divide the dough into several pieces, and mould each piece into an even sausage. Roll out, and, after replacing the stone with a sugar lump and dunking the fruit in apricot liqueur, place an apricot in the middle of each and roll by hand into a dumpling. Place the dumplings in boiling water, and simmer until they rise to the surface. Heat butter and lightly fry the breadcrumbs. Remove the dumplings from the water, drain, and roll in the breadcrumbs. Dust with sugar and serve quickly.

Cream Strudel with Canary Milk

The term "canary milk" is used with intent, since this cream strudel is one of old Vienna's most popular specialities, and in days gone bye, its light yellow milk, coloured by a vanilla pod, was named after those famous feathered singers.

Strudel pastry:
see page 54, stretched apple studel
Filling:
6 bread rolls
approx. ¼ litre milk
100 g (3½ oz) butter
120 g (4 oz) icing sugar
1 lemon, 4 egg yolks
a pinch of salt
¼ litre sour cream
4 egg whites, 60 g (2 oz) raisins
icing sugar
80 g butter, ¼ litre milk
Canary milk:
½ litre milk, 2 egg yolks
1 vanilla pod, 60 g (2 oz) sugar

Remove and discard the crusts of the bread rolls, leave to soften in milk for a while, squeeze and drain. Beat butter until creamy, add sugar, lemon juice, a little grated lemon rind, egg yolks and a pinch of salt. Gradually work in the bread roll mixture and sour cream. Whip egg whites stiffly, and fold into the mixture. Spread this filling on the prepared strudel pastry, sprinkle with raisins, roll up using a cloth, and transfer to a buttered baking tray. Brush with melted butter, and bake in the oven at medium temperature for 50 minutes. After 25 minutes pour over ¼ litre boiling milk. Sprinkle with sugar and serve with canary milk.
Canary milk: whisk milk together with two egg yolks, heat with sugar and vanilla pod, and beat until creamy. Serve hot.

Sliced Spleen Soup

The love affair between Viennese Cuisine and beef soups is easily demonstrated by their sheer variety. Don't be frightened away from this one by the length of time it takes to make the spleen slices: understand instead that here the soup is by no means of secondary importance in a meal.

For the soup:
800 g (1 lb 12 oz) tender beef
200 g (7 oz) beef bones
120 g (4 oz) root vegetables (carrots, celeriac, leek)
1 onion, 6 peppercorns, parsley
50 g (2 oz) beef liver
50 g (2 oz) beef spleen
salt
For the spleen slices:
30 g (1 oz) butter, ½ onion
1 beef spleen
1 teaspoon chopped parsley
salt, pepper
2 eggs
4 slices of white bread
oil for frying, chives

Soup: place meat and thoroughly washed bones in cold water and boil slowly for an hour. Add chopped root vegetables, onion halves with their peel, peppercorns, liver, spleen and salt, and boil over a medium heat for a further 1½ to 2 hours. Strain the finished soup through a cloth.
Spleen slices: heat butter and fry finely chopped onion until golden-yellow. Mash the raw spleen with a fork, season with parsley, salt and pepper, and fry. Stir in the eggs and then allow to cool. Spread the cooled mixture onto slices of bread, and place in the hot oil, meat side down. Turn after three minutes and fry on the other side. Remove, allow to drain on kitchen towel, cut into slices and add to the hot beef soup. Serve sprinkled with parsley.

Palffy Dumplings

To be accurate, the notion of boiling dumplings inside a napkin dates back to the period when Bohemia was part of Austria. This particular dumpling was probably first served in Prague, in the baroque palace of the Barons Palffy. Not until later did it make an appearance in Vienna, but here, in contrast to Bohemia, where they are still served as dessert with sugar and cinammon, they were identified as a savoury accompaniment to meat dishes, above all gulash, *Beuschel* and roast pork.

5 bread rolls
⅛ litre milk
3 eggs
30 g (1 oz) bacon
1 small onion
150 g (5 oz) butter
1 tablespoon chopped parsley
salt
1 tablespoon flour

Slice off crusts, cut rolls into cubes and mash together with a mixture of milk and beaten eggs. Gently fry finely chopped onion and bacon. Beat butter until creamy, and mix thoroughly with the prepared breadcrumbs, bacon, onion, parsley, salt and a tablespoon of flour. Leave to rest, then lay on a dampened, buttered linen napkin, roll into a cylindrical form, and tie the ends of the cloth together firmly with string. Attach the roll to a wooden spoon, and hang into boiling water. Boil for 30 minutes. Dunk briefly in cold water, unwrap, cut into finger-thick slices and serve straight away.

Panadel Soup

It is quite legitimate to draw parallels between *Panadel* Soup and the Italian *panata*. In the end, the difference lies in a very special touch. Parmesan is used for the panata, whereas a Panadel Soup is flavoured with nutmeg.

Nutmeg, originally brought into Europe by Muslim traders from Java, is mainly used in Austria for thickened soups and broths, as well as vegetarian and potato dishes.

A tip: Whole round nutmegs are best. Never store ground nutmeg in plastic containers, only in glass.

---

200 g (7 oz) bread
1½ litre veal stock
1 onion
50 g (2 oz) butter
salt, pepper
nutmeg
⅛ litre cream
1 egg yolk
chives

Slice and remove crust from the bread, then place in simmering veal stock. Beat the soup with a whisk until the bread has entirely disintegrated. Fry finely chopped onion in oil until golden-brown and add to the soup. Season with salt, pepper and nutmeg. Remove the soup from the heat and thicken with the cream and egg yolk. Sprinkle with chives before serving.

Stuffed Green Peppers

Before the fall of the Austro-Hungarian empire, Burgenland was part of the Hungarian Kingdom. The green pepper, now grown around Lake Neusiedler is therefore a Hungarian legacy. In all probability, it came into Europe at the start of the sixteenth century from both East and West. The Turks, Hungary's residents for 150 years, had brought with them an Indian version, planting it for their own needs. This pepper remained as the Turks were beaten back, and is known now as one of the hall marks of Hungarian cuisine.

8 fresh green peppers
50 g (2 oz) butter
1 onion
400 g (14 oz) minced veal
salt, pepper
100 g (3½ oz) boiled rice
50 g (2 oz) butter
1 tablespoon flour
400 g (14 oz) boiled, puréed tomatoes

Slice the tops off the peppers with a sharp knife, remove the cores, and wash them thoroughly inside and out. Heat butter, fry finely chopped onion until golden-brown, add meat and fry briefly before seasoning with salt and pepper, and mixing with the boiled rice. Once this filling has been thoroughly mixed together, pack it into the prepared peppers, and arrange, open ends up on a buttered roasting tray. Make a light roux using butter and flour, and mix in boiled, puréed and salted tomatoes to form a sauce. Pour tomato sauce over the peppers, and leave to cook in an oven at medium temperature for approximately 20 minutes.

Forest-Dwellers' Mushroom Strudel

What pastries and doughnuts are in the West and South of Austria, strudel is in the North-East and East. Begin with apple strudel, keep going, and you will find at least one variety for every letter of the alphabet: sweet and savoury; baked and boiled; stretched, beaten, stirred or kneaded. The Forest-Dwellers' Strudel, made with fresh mushrooms, is a traditional summer dish.

Stretched dough (see recipe for apple strudel, page 54)
50 g (2 oz) butter
1 tablespoon chopped parsley
300 g (11 oz) mushrooms
60 g (2 oz) butter
parsley

Stretch the strudel dough over a napkin. Heat butter, fry parsley and mushrooms, add a little water and stew further, until the mushrooms are soft. Roll the cooled filling into the strudel dough using the napkin, tie the ends of the napkin firmly, and hang in salted, simmering water. Remove and unwrap after roughly 20 minutes, leave to drain, pour melted butter over, sprinkle with parsley and serve straight away.

Styrian Chicken

The word *Poularde* is used for young, fattened chickens, slaughtered before reaching maturity. The famous French *poulets de Bresse* are most similar to the Styrian *Poularde*, which has been exported around the world for the last hundred years as *Poularde de Styria*, and is prepared in the most imaginative of ways.

1 chicken
2 bread rolls
2 eggs
⅛ litre milk
60 g (2 oz) butter
1 chicken liver
1 tablespoon chopped parsley
rosemary
salt
50 g (2 oz) butter
1 tablespoon cognac

Wash and prepare the chicken, then slice open the breast and enlarge the cavity with one hand. Thinly slice bread rolls. Beat eggs and milk together, and pour it over the bread. Leave to rest for approximately ½ hour. In the meantime, thoroughly fry the chicken liver in 20 g (½ oz) butter, and again thinly slice.
Beat 40 g (1½ oz) butter until creamy. Mix well with bread, chicken liver, chopped parsley, rosemary and a little salt. Stuff this mixture into the opened breast and stomach of the chicken. Salt the chicken, pour melted butter over, and roast for roughly an hour in an oven at medium temperature. Baste repeatedly with the meat juices, and trickle a tablespoon of cognac over it. Remove, carve and serve with a green salad.

Smoked Platter

All the specialities of the smoke house, real framer's bacon, smoked beef, black pudding and smoked sausage, are best served on a wooden platter. A well heaped wooden platter, strong root schnapps or the striking juniper berry schnapps: all you could desire for a *Jause*, a *Neuner*, a *Znüni*, a *Marend*, a *Gabelfrühstück*, or whatever other names the Austrians have for a snack between meals. Lumberjacks invented the wooden platter by cutting out nice round plates from the freshly felled pine trees, so as to cut their break bacon on them. The more the scent of resin remained, the more popular were the plates.

8 slices each of:
bacon
smoked beef
black pudding or smoked sausage
gherkins
radishes
2 tablespoons horseradish
150 g (5 oz) butter
salt
lemon juice
1 tablespoon ground juniper berries

Attractively arrange the smoked meat and serve with gherkins, radishes, and freshly grated horseradish. Beat butter until creamy, then flavour with salt, lemon juice and freshly ground juniper berries. Serve with rough wholemeal bread or rye bread rolls.

Smoked Tongue with Dill Potatoes

The same dill that lends its particular flavour to our potatoes, was already in common use among the ancient Egyptians as a medicinal ingredient for superstitious spells: "Lay in my slipper, a bunch of dill, and the son-in-law shall do my will," chanted the mother of the bride on her way to the church.

The stalks of the dill plant grow to over one metre in height. Both the plant and the seeds are used as herbs.

---

1 smoked beef tongue
100 g (3½ oz) root vegetables
1 small onion
60 g (2 oz) butter
40 g (1½ oz) flour
1 litre beef stock
1 bunch of dill
lemon rind
salt, pepper
a splash of vinegar
⅛ litre sour cream
1 kg (2¼ lb) potatoes

Slowly boil beef tongue in water with root vegetables until tender. Fry onions in melted butter, then stir in flour to make a light gravy base. Pour in stock and season with finely chopped dill, grated lemon peel, salt, pepper and a splash of vinegar. Boil into a smooth sauce and then add sour cream. Add potatoes, bring quickly to the boil and simmer for a few minutes. Remove tongue from water, peel outer skin away and cut into slanted, finger-thick slices before laying across the dill potatoes. Serve straight away.

Trauttmansdorff Rice Cake

This dish commemorates the Austrian states-
man, Baron Ferdinand Trauttmansdorff, and
tastes best when made with fresh raspberries. It was the recommendation of Alber-
tus Magnus that fresh raspberries always be
eaten as a starter, but you won't need them
here. This moulded rice desert captivates all
those with a sweet tooth.

½ litre milk
125 g (4½ oz) rice
¼ vanilla pod
½ teaspoon grated lemon rind
pinch salt
6 leaves of gelatine
80 g (3 oz) sugar
200 g (7 oz) fresh raspberries
4 tablespoons Maraschino
¼ litre whipped cream
oil
100 g (3½ oz) raspberries

Heat milk, add rice, vanilla, lemon peel and
a pinch of salt, then remove the vanilla.
Leave gelatine for 5 minutes in cold water to
soften, then drain and stir into the boiled
rice, adding sugar. Leave to cool before
folding in first raspberries, steeped in Maraschino, and then carefully the stiffly whipped
cream. Brush a ring mould with oil, fill it
with the mixture, and place in the fridge.
Remove after an hour and turn out, garnishing with raspberries and a little cream, and
serving with fresh raspberry purée.

Beef Salad

The beef stock required for so many of these recipes leaves us with a surplus of boiled beef. Some might say far too much. Hence, a whole host of different people have given time and thought to what can be made with the smaller leftovers or pieces of soup beef. This beef salad was one idea. It can be eaten either as a starter or a middle course, or served as a main dish for an evening meal.

400 g (14 oz) boiled beef
1 onion
2 gherkins
1 tablespoon capers
salt, pepper
vinegar
oil
3 hard boiled eggs
1 red and 1 green pepper
1 onion
chives

Remove beef from the stock, leave on grease-proof paper to drain and cool completely. Thinly slice the meat, finely chop onion, gherkins and capers, mix thoroughly, season with salt and pepper, and cover with a dressing of vinegar and oil.
Arrange in a glass bowl, garnished with slices of boiled egg, red and green pepper and onion rings, sprinkle with chives, and serve with chive butter bread rolls.

Sacher Torte

The recipe for *Sachertorte*, created by Franz Sacher in 1832, threw all Vienna into the strangest confusion a hundred years later. One of the relatives of the inventor sold his recipe, and a struggle began between the famous Sacher Hotel and Demel Bakers over the copyright. Only in 1962, after a long drawn out court battle, was settlement reached. The Sacher Hotel has since been in possession of the original recipe, and imprints its shield on the chocolate icing. Demellian *Sachertorte* has to be content with the title *Demel-Sachertorte*. Hence, this recipe, like all recipes for *Sachertorte*, is an adaptation.

---

150 g (5 oz) chocolate, 150 g (5 oz) butter
100 g (3½ oz) icing sugar
6 egg yolks, 6 egg whites
50 g (2 oz) sugar, 150 g (5 oz) flour
pinch of salt, apricot conserve
Icing:
200 g (7 oz) chocolate
200 g (7 oz) sugar, ⅛ litre water

Soften chocolate over hot water in a bain-marie, beat with butter until creamy, then stir in egg yolks and icing sugar. Whip egg whites and the sugar until stiff. Fold egg whites and flour – with a pinch of salt – alternately into the chocolate. Pour the mixture into a buttered and floured cake tin, and bake for 1½ hours in an oven at medium temperature, leaving the oven door ajar for the first ten minutes. Turn out and allow to cool, then spread conserve over the top of the cake and cover with the chocolate icing. For the icing, heat water and sugar until it begins to fizz, then carefully stir in chocolate which has again been softened over hot water. Pour over the cake and spread straight away.

Metternich Salad

In the words of some early nineteenth century chefs, "Klemens Lothar Wenzel Baron von Metternich, Lord over Metternich-Winneburg since 1813, has achieved the Holy Alliance between Russia, England, Prussia and Austria. Let us name a salad after him, so that chicken, apple, celeriac and truffles join forces equally wonderfully." Evidently, the salad lasted longer than either the alliance or the Baron's waning popularity. He died in 1859, more unloved than honoured for all his importance.

2 large cooking apples
1 celeriac
juice of 1 lemon
salt, pepper
1 tablespoon mustard
a little sugar
4 tablespoons mayonnaise
1 boiled chicken
1 head lettuce
2 tomatoes
tinned truffles

Peel apple and celeriac which has been boiled in lemon water until soft. Slice thinly and mix thoroughly with salt, pepper, sugar and mayonnaise. Leave to rest in a cool place. Strip the meat from the boiled chicken, again slice thinly, and mix with the apple and celeriac.
Serve in a glass bowl, on a bed of thoroughly washed lettuce, garnish with quatered tomatoes, and sprinkle with a few chopped truffles.

Salonbeuscherl

The little known words *Beuschel* or *Beushl* or *Beuscherl* cloak a combination of veal lung and heart. Only in the twentieth century was it embraced by highter society, and a version prepared with particular care has therefore since been christened *Salonbeuscherl*.

---

800 g (1 lb & 12 oz) veal lung and heart
root vegetables (carrots, celeriac, leek)
1 onion, 1 bayleaf, parsley
peppercorns
thyme, salt
60 g (2 oz) butter
60 g (2 oz) flour
pinch sugar
2 gherkins
1 teaspoon capers, 1 anchovy
1 small onion, 1 clove of garlic
parsley
1 teaspoon wine vinegar
1 tablespoon mustard
lemon juice, vinegar
marjoram
2 tablespoons cream
2 tablespoons meat stock

Place veal lung and heart with the coarsely chopped root vegetables, halved onion, bayleaf, peppercorns, thyme and salt in approximately 2½ litres cold water. Boil for one hour, or until tender, then remove the meat and leave to cool in salted cold water. Fry butter, flour and a pinch of sugar until golden-brown. Finely chop gherkins, capers, anchovy, onion, garlic and parsley, add to the frying-pan, splash with a little vinegar and pour in the Beuschel stock. Boil the sauce for half an hour, then pour over the sliced Beuschel. Bring to the boil again, flavour with mustard, lemon juice, vinegar and some marjoram. Season with cream, and pour hot gulash stock over the middle of the prepared Beuscherl. Side-dish: Palffy dumplings, polenta or semolina dumplings.

Salzburger Nockerln

"As sweet as love, and delicate as a kiss..."
As the story goes, this famed and celebrated
Nockerln was first created around 1600
for Salzburg's Archbishop Wolf Dietrich.
Maybe. Maybe not. This Archbishop, whose
mistress Salome Alt gave birth to fifteen of
his children, and for whom he built Castle
Mirabell, has certainly gone down in culinary
history as a gourmet, but the *Nockerln* of
that period looked entirely different to our
modern version. Nor was the vanilla pod
introduced to Austria until some time later.

5 egg whites
30 g (1 oz) sugar
3 egg yolks
1 packet of vanilla sugar
lemon rind
20 g (½ oz) flour
30 g (1 oz) butter
1 tablespoon sugar
4 tablespoons milk or cream
vanilla sugar

Beat egg whites until very stiff, and fold in
first sugar, then carefully the egg yolks,
vanilla sugar, a little grated lemon peel and
flour. Shape three, pyramide-like Nockerln
from the mixture, and place on a buttered,
ovenproof tray, sprinkled with sugar. Bake in
the oven at medium temperature for 5 minutes. Then from the side, pour in milk,
mixed with vanilla sugar, and bake for a further 3–4 minutes. The Nockerln should
remain a little creamy in the middle. As soon
as they are removed from the oven, sprinkle
with sugar, and serve from the ovenproof
tray.

Pig's Snout with Lentils

A tradional New Year's Eve supper, based on the biblical story related by Moses, so that even as Esau exchanged his pastures for a dish of lentils, the old year is exchanged for the new.

On New Year's Eve, Austrians wish to beseech the Powers of Good, and, because they are gourmets, they do this with knife and fork. The pig's snout symbolizes good luck, the lentils wealth for a whole year, and the horseradish health.

2 pork snouts
salt
200 g (7 oz) root vegetables (carrot, celeriac, leek)
1 small onion, parsley
1 bayleaf
peppercorns
juniper berries
400 g (14 oz) lentils
50 g (2 oz) butter
2 tablespoons freshly grated horseradish

Boil pig's snouts with sliced root vegetables and onion rings until tender. Boil lentils, then drain the water, and mix in fresh butter. Carefully remove all meat from the pig's snouts, arrange nicely, sprinkle with horseradish, and serve with the lentils.

Ham and Pasta Bake

Like a little piece of Vienna: the gastronomical regionalism celebrated with this dish is certainly coming back with a vengeance! This earns the Viennese seal of approval for any housewife, for the cook of a rustic tavern, or for a wine cellar serving hot dishes. Woe to any chef with the bright idea of using leftovers from yesterday's roast rather than ham.

200 g (7 oz) pasta
salt
80 g butter
2 egg yolks
salt, pepper
nutmeg
250 g (9 oz) boiled ham
⅛ litre sour cream
2 egg whites
butter
breadcrumbs

Boil pasta in salted water for 8–10 minutes, drain, briefly dunk in cold water, and leave to drip thoroughly. Beat egg yolks with butter until creamy, season with salt, pepper and a little nutmeg. Add the pasta and finely cubed ham, and mix thoroughly with sour cream. Beat egg whites until stiff and stir into the mixture. Brush an ovenproof bowl with butter and sprinkle with breadcrumbs. Add the mixture, and sprinkle with a few butter slices and breadcrumbs. Bake in the oven at medium temperature for ¾ hour until golden-brown. Serve with a green salad, either directly from the ovenproof dish, or cut into portions.

Tyrolean Schlutz Pastries

There are dozens of recipes instructing how to fill *Schlutz*, *Schlick* or *Schlipf* pastries: with minced meat or finely chopped brain, with cabbage and bacon or curd cheese, with jam or prunes. *Schlutz* pastries are eaten "at sea or on dry land," meaning either in or out of a soup. One of the most popular Tyrolean recipes fills them with seasoned spinach. Hence they are occasionally called spinach pastries.

400 g (14 oz) rye flour
100 g (3½ oz) wheat flour
1 egg
3 tablespoons oil, salt
approximately ½ litre luke-warm water
Filling: 500 g (1 lb) spinach
40 g (1½ oz) butter
1 small onion
1 tablespoon chopped parsley
1 tablespoon flour
1 tablespoon milk
nutmeg, salt
Seasoning: 50 g (2 oz) grated cheese
50 g (2 oz) butter

Mix and knead together flour, egg, oil, salt and water to form a smooth dough, roll out thinly, and, using a glass or a pastry cutter, cut out 6–7 cm wide circles. Boil spinach in salted water, then drain. Heat butter and add finely chopped onion and parsley, mix in flour, allow to cook slightly, then salt, dowse with milk, season and mix with drained spinach.

Place a spoonful of spinach in the centre of each pastry, fold together, and press the edges firmly together. Place the pastries in boiling salted water, and, as soon as they rise to the surface, remove and leave to drain before sprinkling with grated cheese and pouring melted butter over.

Pierced Escargot

During ages when the observance of fast days in Austria was on the increase – at one time reaching a total of 148 days in the year – the popularity of snails had a tendency to grow and grow. It is most obvious during the Roman era, when snails were first bred, and re-appeared in the monasteries of the Middle Ages where the same idea was continued. In the lush pastures of Lower Eastern Austria, snails are so abundant, that every year hundreds of tonnes are exported to France. As observance of fast days slackened, snails virtually vanished from the menu. Despite this, it is undoubtedly worth the effort to try and prepare snails "like Grandma".

4 dozen escargots, fresh or tinned
1 bayleaf
thyme
salt, pepper
garlic
40 g (1½ oz) butter
Batter:
125 g (4½ oz) flour
⅛ litre white wine
salt
2 eggs
1 tablespoon oil
oil for frying
parsley
1 lemon

Boil snails in lightly salted water with bayleaf and thyme, remove and allow to cool. Season with salt, pepper and garlic, and fry gently in butter. Make a smooth batter using flour, white wine, salt, eggs and oil. Pierce the cooled snails with cocktail sticks, pull them through the batter, and fry in oil until golden-brown. Garnish with parsley and slices of lemon. Serve with lettuce and sauce tartare.

Chantarelle Gulash

One of the ancient masters of Hungarian cuisine, Karoly Gundel, once commented: "without wishing to offend my foreign colleagues, I must say that they are no credit to the creation of fine goulash." With his outlook on the world, he must be seen to have been correct, but once gulash – or *Golasch* – had emigrated, it was so embraced by the Austrians that they were reluctant to part with it even during Lent. Instead of beef, pork or veal, they simply used chantarelle mushrooms.

80 g butter
1 tablespoon chopped parsley
1 kg (2¼ lb) chantarelle mushrooms
salt, pepper
a little paprika
40 g (1½ oz) flour
¼ litre sour cream

Fry chopped parsley lightly in hot butter, add small, thoroughly washed and halved chantarelles, salt, pepper, sprinkle with a little paprika, and stew until soft. At the end, dust with flour and cook briefly before dowsing with a little water. Return to the boil and stir in sour cream and seasoning.
A good accompaniment: sliced dumpling, with fried eggs laid on top.

Maidens in their Nightgowns

For over a century, pork has been one of our major sources of meat. Quite unfairly, despite an enormous variety of seasonings, and even when prepared with great care, pork has only very rarely succeeded in breaking into the elite band of haute cuisine. However, meet this maiden, the fillet. Wrap the succulent morsel in a nightgown of puff pastry, embraced by delicate mushrooms.

1 packet frozen puff pastry
1 pork fillet
40 g (1½ oz) butter
pepper
ground rosemary
salt
40 g (1½ oz) butter
1 tablespoon chopped parsley
300 g (11 oz) mushrooms
20 g (½ oz) flour
4 slices of ham
1 egg

Defrost puff pastry and roll out until approximately 1 mm thick. Fry fillet in butter until almost cooked through, and season with pepper, rosemary, and salt. Remove from the pan and allow to cool. Heat butter, lightly fry parsley, add washed and sliced mushrooms, fry until soft, and then drape over the fillet.

Spread ham on the rolled pastry, and wrap the fillet so that the edges of the pastry, pressed together with water, are lying flat. Place on a buttered tray, decorate with the pastry leftovers, and pierce. Brush the surface with beaten egg, and bake the "Maiden" in the oven for approximately 25 minutes at a high temperature. Serve with a cabbage salad.

Celeriac in Wine Batter

When celeriac first appeared as a cultured plant in the German speaking territories under Karl the Great, it had already travelled through several historical millenia. The Ancient Egyptians revered it, the Greeks called it *selinon* and founded Selinunt with a leaf of celeriac as coat of arms, the Romans called it God of the Underworld and planted it on graves. Today it is still important to us, the stalks and leaves containing essential vitamins and minerals.

2–3 celeriacs depending on their size
lemon
salt
2 eggs
⅛ litre wine
150 g (5 oz) flour
oil for frying

Cut celeriacs into finger-thick slices, and boil in salted water with a splash of lemon juice. Then remove and leave to drain completely. Make a smooth wine batter using eggs, wine and flour, dip the celeriac slices in it, and fry quickly, swimming in oil. Serve straight away with sauce tartare and thinly sliced ham.

Tyrolean Bacon Dumplings

The older, more elaborate cookery books of the gentry made no space for bacon dumplings. In aristocratic households they were not au fait, and even the common cook books referred to them using the diminutive *Knöderl*, pushing them to the side of the plate as a mere addition to soups. Revenge is now sweet, since none of the recipes for soup dumplings can do justice to the original Tyrolean Bacon Dumpling, that which, with a little imagination, can be seen as imprinted on a twelfth century fresco in Hocheppan. A Tyrolean housewife's tip: "tak' a muckl' big slab o' bacon!"

400 g (14 oz) bacon
100 g (3½ oz) smoked sausage
500 g (1 lb) white bread or chopped bread rolls
5 eggs
¼ litre milk
1 tablespoon chopped parsley
flour
salt

Cut bacon and smoked sausage into small cubes, and mix with bread. Beat eggs with milk, add chopped parsley and pour over the bacon-bread mixture. Mix, leave for 10 minutes, then bind with flour and salt.
With wet hands shape into dumplings, and boil slowly for 10–15 minutes in salted water. It is advisable to test first a single dumpling, in order to insure that the dough is neither too loose nor too firm. The first case can be resolved by adding some more flour or bread, the latter by adding milk. Another down to earth serving tip: Let th' first dumplin' be eaten wi' soup, th' secn'd wi' cabbage, and th' next wi' salad."

Rump of Beef with Apple and Horseradish

A hundred years ago, there were already twenty-two official Viennese quality classes for oxen. This was the start of a veritable beef cult, as correct preparation of the juicy Hungarian fattened or grazing cattle into *Tafelspitzen, Kavalierspitzen, Schulterscherzeln* and eighteen other almost incomprehensible varieties, became the source of bitter culinary wars. The boiling of beef alone divided gourmets into thirteen different camps. Since Emperor Franz Josef was one of the most vehement advocates of boiled rump, this appetizing dish has gained greatest fame.

1½ kg (3½ lb) prime rump of beef
½ onion
1 carrot
1 finger long piece leek
1 bunch parsley
1 slice celeriac
8 peppercorns
salt
Apple & horseradish:
3 large apples, 1 lemon
salt, a little sugar
2 tablespoons freshly grated horseradish
chives

Place rump of beef in a large quantity of boiling water. Finely chop and briefly fry the onion. After half an hour, add it to the meat, with peeled but whole vegetables, salt and peppercorns. Boil at a medium temperature for 2 hours. Remove the cooked beef from the soup, slice across the grain, arrange on a serving dish, topped with some of the stock, and garnished with chives and vegetables.
Apple and horseradish: peel, core and grate apples, then serve immediately, mixed with the lemon juice, salt, a pinch of sugar and the grated horseradish. Side dish: sautéd potatoes.

False Tuna

The capers and the anchovies that play such an important role in this recipe, were introduced to the Austrian cuisine during the 18th century. Since then there has been a wide variety of recipes featuring the two ingredients, and anchovies in particular are indispensible in the traditional Austrian recipes.

Of all the five varieties of capers, *Nonpareilles*, *Surfines*, *Fines*, *Mifines* and *Communes*, the small *Nonpareilles* are held to be the best.

---

500 g (1 lb) joint of veal
1 bayleaf
peppercorns
salt
1 carrot
1 bunch of parsley
6 anchovies
2 tablespoons capers
⅛ litre oil

Place the joint of veal in hot water, add herbs and vegetables and boil slowly until cooked through. Remove meat from the stock, and leave to cool. Chop the anchovies finely, add capers and mix well with the oil.

Thinly slice the cooled veal, lay on a flat plate, and cover with the anchovy sauce. Leave in a cool place for twelve hours. Then remove the meat from the marinade, leave to drain a little, then arrange on top of a green salad – garnished with a mushroom dressing, made with hard boiled eggs, tomato and mayonnaise – and serve.

Curd Cheese Dumplings with Fried Plums

There are no tigers in Austria, only a species of bi-ped named *Mehlspeistiger*, because he falls on all sweet dishes with a true passion. There are however sweet dishes (in Austrian cuisine called *Mehlspeisen* which means flour dishes), that include no flour, like the rice cake. And, there are sweet dishes which aren't even sweet, like *Teigfleckerln*, in addition to a variety in which white bread replaces the flour. Curd cheese dumplings belong to this last group.

60 g (2 oz) butter, 4 eggs, 100 g (3½ oz) sugar
vanilla sugar, lemon juice, pinch salt
120 g (4 oz) white bread
500 g (1 lb) curd cheese
2 tablespoons sour cream, 50 g (2 oz) butter
100 g (3½ oz) breadcrumbs, icing sugar
Fried plums: ½ kg (1 lb) plums
10 g (⅓ oz) sugar, cinnamon, lemon juice, rum

Beat butter with eggs, sugar, vanilla sugar and a pinch of salt until creamy. Cut crusts off white bread and cube. Add to the creamy curd cheese, fold in sour cream and stir into the butter mixture. Leave the finished dough to rest in a cool place for one hour. Then, with wet hands form small dumplings, place in boiling salted water and simmer, half covered for approximately 10 minutes. Remove the finished dumplings, leave to drain on greaseproof paper, roll carefully in breadcrumbs, fry in butter, and sprinkle with icing sugar.

Fried plums: Halve ripe plums, remove stones, then in a heated sauce pan with sugar, cinnamon, some lemon juice and a teaspoon of rum, stir until the skins start to roll away, and the fruit begins to disintegrate.

Curd Cream Pancakes

A tip on how to prepare wafer-thin pancakes without running any risk that they fall apart: bake each pancake in the oven, and remove simply by slanting the tray onto a piece of aluminium foil. Wrap the pancake in the foil, and pile one on top of the other. To lift each pancake just raise the foil, fill and roll.

6 eggs
¼ litre milk
⅛ litre soda water
4 tablespoons flour
pinch salt
butter for baking
Filling: 40 g (1½ oz) butter
50 g (2 oz) icing sugar
3 egg yolks
300 g (11 oz) curd cheese
3 tablespoons sour cream
60 g (2 oz) raisins
lemon peel
1 packet vanilla sugar
3 egg whites
⅛ litre milk, 1 egg
vanilla sugar, icing sugar

Make a smooth, runny batter using eggs, milk, soda water, flour and salt. Heat butter on a flat baking tray, pour over one ladle full (approximately ⅛ litre), and spread evenly. Bake in the oven until golden yellow.
Filling: Beat butter with egg yolks and icing sugar until creamy, and mix with drained curd cheese, sour cream, raisins, a little grated lemon peel, and stiffly beaten egg whites.
Fill the pancakes, and either roll, or fold into triangles, then lay in a buttered, ovenproof tray, and bake for a few minutes in the oven. Beat together milk, egg and sugar, pour over the pancakes and continue baking for a further 20 minutes. Serve sprinkled with sugar.

Styrian Potted Bacon

Garlic, or as the Styrians say *Knofel*, which plays such an important role in potted meats, was first mentioned in connection with the Emperor Nero. This cruel Roman gorged himself on it in order to improve his singing voice. Apparently the doctor's order missed its mark, since it is written that "he still yowled like a cat on heat," and hence the advice given by Roman epigram writer Martial seems to make sense: "If you have eaten garlic . . . keep your mouth closed when kissing."

500 g (1 lb) smoked bacon
salt, pepper
porkfat
garlic

Remove the rind, and cut bacon into very small – pea-sized – pieces. Salt, pepper, mix well and press into an earthenware pot, brushed with fat. Heat a little pork fat and pour over the surface of the bacon. Cover with a linen cloth, and leave to ripen in a cool place for approximately three weeks. Serve as a spread with a lot of garlic and black bread.

Poached Catfish with Almonds

Catfish can grow to three metres in length and weigh up to 25 kg. This largest of all sweet water fish is therefore an extremely plump individual and packs its wide mouth mainly with crabs, fish, frogs and water fowl. In Austria it is found especially in the Danube. Anglers prefer the younger fishes, since their meat is still very white and succulent.

1 onion, parsley
150 g (5 oz) root vegetables (carrot, celeriac, leek)
40 g (1½ oz) butter
800 g (1 lb & 12 oz) sliced catfish
salt, pepper
1 bayleaf
½ litre white wine
80 g butter
100 g (3½ oz) chopped almonds
⅛ litre cream
1 tablespoon chopped parsley

Fry onion rings and finely chopped root vegetables in butter, and place them in an ovenproof dish. Layer catfish slices on top, seasoned with salt and pepper, add bayleaf and pour over white wine. Poach in the oven at a medium temperature. Remove the slices of catfish from the dish and keep warm. Fry chopped almonds in a little butter until golden yellow, then dowse with the cream, bring briefly to the boil and pour over the catfish slices. Serve sprinkled with parsley. Boiled potatoes are a suitable accompaniment.

Wiener Schnitzel

One piece history gave birth to a host of histories: Field Marshall Baron Radetzky, grimly determined to keep Lombardy within Austria, even against the wishes of rebellious Lombardians, not only sent military reports to his King but also a Lombard cook, who would betray the secrets of the *Costoletta Milanese* to the Austrian chefs. Austria lost Lombardy in 1859, but the Viennese at least annexed the *Schnitzel*, which then marched to conquering victory through the kitchens of the whole world as the *Wiener Schnitzel*, and can be found in a whole variety of different – and unappealing – forms.

4 veal schnitzels (from the leg)
salt
200 g (7 oz) flour
2 eggs
2 tablespoons milk
200 g (7 oz) breadcrumbs
fat or oil for frying
lemon
parsley

Pound schnitzels lightly, salt, turn in flour, pull through a mixture of beaten eggs and milk, and press lightly on both sides into the breadcrumbs. Immediately after coating, fry the schnitzels, swimming in hot fat or oil, until golden brown. After frying, leave to drain for a few moments on greaseproof paper, garnish with slices of lemon and parsley, and serve straight away.
A mixed or potato salad should be served with Wiener Schnitzel.

Viennese Washing Maids

Washing Maids are a Viennese speciality of days gone bye. Then they were sharp rather than sweet, coquettish rather than shy, plump rather than slim. These sturdy, healthy maids may indeed have given the creator of this pudding inspiration for a name. After all, washing maids were said to be somewhat like East Austrian apricots: "A wee bit sharp, very tasty and wi' a hidden sweet centre."

Batter:
150 g (5 oz) flour
⅛ litre white wine
2 egg yolks
20 g (½ oz) oil
pinch of salt
2 egg whites
20 g (½ oz) icing sugar
16 ripe apricots
150 g (5 oz) marzipan
2 tablespoons apricot liqueur
icing sugar
oil for deep frying
vanilla sugar

Mix flour, wine, egg yolks, oil and salt to form a smooth batter. Beat egg whites with sugar until stiff, and fold carefully into the batter. Wash and peel apricots, remove stones, and replace with a ball of marzipan. Sprinkle with sugar and dribble over a little apricot liqueur. Leave to rest for a few moments, then dip the apricots in batter, deep fry in hot oil until golden brown, and serve sprinkled with vanilla sugar.

Carp with Vegetables and Horseradish

Carp were known in Austria in Iron Age times, but it was not until the Middle Ages that the monasteries, often situated at great distances from a river, began to build fish farms in order to have a source of fish for themselves, and later to breed them. The Lower Austrian Monastery of Zwettl for example, has bred carp since the early 16th century, and hence it is hardly a surprise that a cookery book written in 1719 by the court chef of the Salzburg Archbishop, contains a total of seven different recipes for the fish. Nowadays, and especially on Christmas Eve, carp is served in almost every Austrian household.

1 kg (2¼ lb) carp
250 g (9 oz) root vegetables (carrot, celeriac, leek)
1 onion, parsley
1 clove of garlic
salt, peppercorns
bayleaf
thyme
a little sugar
2 tablespoons wine vinegar

Cut the carp into portion-sized pieces. Place with finely chopped root vegetables, chopped garlic and onion, in a broad saucepan with quite high sides, season, cover with water and wine vinegar – the carp must be completely covered by liquid – and boil slowly until tender. Arrange the fish on a preheated serving platter, sprinkle generously with the chopped vegetables and serve with boiled potatoes and freshly grated horseradish.

The Recipes According to Groups

Unless otherwise stated, the amounts given are for four servings.

Photographs

Bibliothèque Nationale, Brussels: 13 – Geiersperger/Merten: 6/7, 32 t. l.
Kunsthistorisches Museum, Vienna: 15
Lessing/laenderpress: 8/9, 45 (Nationalmuseum, Budapest),
46/47 (Historisches Museum of Vienna)
Löbl-Schreyer: 2, 10/11, 22/23, 28/29, 32 t. r., 32 b. l.,33 (3), 36(6), 37, 39, 42 t. l., 42 b. r.,
42/43 (large picture)
C. L. Schmitt: 26/27 – Pronto/Mauritius: 38 – roebild/Assmann: 42 t. r., 42 b. l.
Sirius Bildarchiv/Döbbelin: 50/51, 54–203 – Sirius Bildarchiv/G. Schmidt: 24/25
Staatliche Kunstsammlungen, Dresden, Gemäldegalerie Alte Meister/Gerhard Reinhold: 49
Theatermuseum, Munich/Joachim-Blauel-Artothek: 18/19

Culinary Tours

The following have already been published
in the same series.
Also available in Englisch
Dine around the world, Switzerland, Germany, and *Swabia*.

OSTERN

NUDELN

BIER

AKTIV & VITAL

MIKROWELLE

THÜRINGEN
Kulinarische Streifzüge

BADEN
Kulinarische Streifzüge

BAYERN
Kulinarische Streifzüge

SCHWABEN
Kulinarische Streifzüge

SACHSEN
Kulinarische Streifzüge

SCHWEIZ
Kulinarische Streifzüge

FRANKREICH
Kulinarische Streifzüge

ÖSTERREICH
Kulinarische Streifzüge

EUROPA
Kulinarische Streifzüge

CHINA
Kulinarische Streifzüge